About This Book

Why This Book Is Important

This third book in the M&E Series explores the techniques that can be used to isolate the effects of programs on business measures from the effects of other factors. Many factors can affect business performance; some are direct effects of the program, and others are not. Top organizations use the techniques in this book to isolate the program effects of a variety of programs, an important step in measuring return on investment.

A direct cause-and-effect relationship between a program and business performance can be difficult to prove, but it can be accomplished. This book shows how up-front planning can ensure that this important step in program evaluation is accomplished successfully. It also discusses why isolation of program effects is important.

What This Book Achieves

This book shows how to isolate the effects of a program from other influences, using the following techniques:

- Control groups

- Trend lines and forecasts

- Expert estimates

In addition, this volume explains how to select the appropriate technique for any situation and any level of evaluation.

How This Book Is Organized

This book begins with a brief introduction to the ROI process model and the Twelve Guiding Principles. Chapter One discusses why isolating program effects is so important.

The book then introduces and describes the techniques that can be used to isolate the effects of a program. Chapter Two examines the use of control groups, which is the most credible way to isolate the effects of a program. This chapter also describes many of the issues surrounding this technique and includes several examples of how organizations have used control groups.

Chapter Three discusses another method of isolating the effects of a program: trend line analysis and forecasting. Several case examples are provided to illustrate the use of these methods. Chapter Four examines the least credible way to isolate the effects of a program: estimates. The chapter discusses possible sources of expert input, including program participants, participants' immediate managers, senior management, customers, and experts. Several case examples show how estimates can be used to isolate the effects of the program.

In Chapter Five, a matching exercise illustrates situations that are appropriate for each method. The importance of isolating program effects is discussed once again, along with several myths surrounding this issue. How to build credibility into the process of isolating program effects is also examined.

The Measurement and Evaluation Series

Editors

Patricia Pulliam Phillips, Ph.D.

Jack J. Phillips, Ph.D.

Introduction to the Measurement and Evaluation Series

The ROI Six Pack provides detailed information on developing ROI evaluations, implementing the ROI Methodology, and showing the value of a variety of functions and processes. With detailed examples, tools, templates, shortcuts, and checklists, this series will be a valuable reference for individuals interested in using the ROI Methodology to show the impact of their projects, programs, and processes.

The Need

Although financial ROI has been measured for over one hundred years to quantify the value of plants, equipment, and companies, the concept has only recently been applied to evaluate the impact of learning and development, human resources, technology, quality, marketing, and other support functions. In the learning and development field alone, the use of ROI has become routine in many organizations. In the past decade, hundreds of organizations have embraced the ROI process to show the impact of many different projects and programs.

Along the way, professionals and practitioners need help. They need tools, templates, and tips, along with explanations, examples, and details, to make this process work. Without this help, using the ROI Methodology to show the value of projects and programs is difficult. In short, practitioners need shortcuts and proven techniques to minimize the resources required to use this process. Practitioners' needs have created the need for this series. This series will provide the detail necessary to make the ROI Methodology successful within an organization. For easy reference and use, the books are logically arranged to align with the steps of the ROI Methodology.

Audience

The principal audience for these books is individuals who plan to use the ROI Methodology to show the value of their projects and programs. Such individuals are specialists or managers charged with proving the value of their particular project or program. They need detailed information, know-how, and confidence.

A second audience is those who have used the ROI Methodology for some time but want a quick reference with tips and techniques to make ROI implementation more successful within their organization. This series, which explains the evaluation process in detail, will be a valuable reference set for these individuals, regardless of other ROI publications owned.

A third audience is consultants and researchers who want to know how to address specific evaluation issues. Three important challenges face individuals as they measure ROI and conduct ROI evaluations: (1) collecting post-program data, (2) isolating the effects of the program, and (3) converting data to monetary values. A book is devoted to each of these critical issues, allowing researchers and consultants to easily find details on each issue.

A fourth audience is those who are curious about the ROI Methodology and its use. The first book in this series focuses specifically on ROI, its use, and how to determine whether it is appropriate for an organization. When interest is piqued, the remaining books provide more detail.

Flow of the Books

The six books are presented in a logical sequence, mirroring the ROI process model. Book one, *ROI Fundamentals: Why and When to Measure ROI*, presents the basic ROI Methodology and makes the business case for measuring ROI as it explores the benefits and barriers to implementation. It also examines the type of organization best suited for the ROI Methodology and the best time to implement it. Planning for an ROI evaluation is also explored in this book.

Book two, *Data Collection: Planning For and Collecting All Types of Data*, details data collection by examining the different techniques, methods, and issues involved in this process, with an emphasis on collecting post-program data. It examines the different data collection methods: questionnaires, interviews, focus groups, observation, action plans, performance contracts, and monitoring records.

Book three, *Isolation of Results: Defining the Impact of the Program*, focuses on the most valuable part of the ROI Methodology and the essential step for ensuring credibility. Recognizing that factors other than the program being measured can influence results, this book shows a variety of ways in which the effects of a program can be isolated from other influences. Techniques include comparison analysis using a control group, trend line analysis and forecasting methods, and expert input from a variety of sources.

Book four, *Data Conversion: Calculating the Monetary Benefits*, covers perhaps the second toughest challenge of ROI evaluation: placing monetary value on program benefits. To calculate the ROI, data must be converted to money, and *Data Conversion* shows how this conversion has been accomplished in a variety of organizations. The good news is that standard values are available for many items. When they are not, the book shows different techniques for converting them, ranging from calculating the value from records to seeking experts and searching databases. When data cannot be converted to money credibly and with minimum resources, they are considered intangible. This book explores the range of intangible benefits and the necessary techniques for collecting, analyzing, and recording them.

Book five, *Costs and ROI: Evaluating at the Ultimate Level*, focuses on costs and ROI. This book shows that all costs must be captured in order to create a fully loaded cost profile. All the costs must be included in order to be conservative and to give the analysis additional credibility. Next, the actual ROI calculation is presented, showing the various assumptions and issues that must be addressed when calculating the ROI. Three different calculations are presented: the benefit-cost ratio, the ROI percentage, and the payback period. The book concludes with several cautions and concerns about the use of ROI and its meaning.

Book six, *Communication and Implementation: Sustaining the Practice*, explores two important issues. The first issue is reporting the results of an evaluation. This is the final part of the ROI Methodology and is necessary to ensure that audiences have the information they need so that improvement processes can be implemented. A range of techniques is available, including face-to-face meetings, brief reports, one-page summaries, routine communications, mass-audience techniques, and electronic media. All are available for reporting evaluation results. The final part of the book focuses on how to sustain the ROI evaluation process: how to use it, keep it going, and make it work in the long term to add value to the organization and, often, to show the value of all the programs and projects within a function or department.

Terminology: Programs, Projects, Solutions

In this series the terms *program* and *project* are used to describe many processes that can be evaluated using the ROI Methodology. This is an important issue because readers may vary widely in their perspectives. Individuals involved in technology applications may

Table I.1. Terms and Applications

Term	Example
Program	Leadership development skills enhancement for senior executives
Project	A reengineering scheme for a plastics division
System	A fully interconnected network for all branches of a bank
Initiative	A faith-based effort to reduce recidivism
Policy	A new preschool plan for disadvantaged citizens
Procedure	A new scheduling arrangement for truck drivers
Event	A golf outing for customers
Meeting	A U.S. Coast Guard conference on innovations
Process	Quality sampling
People	Staff additions in the customer care center
Tool	A new means of selecting hotel staff

use the terms *system* and *technology* rather than *program* or *project*. In public policy, in contrast, the word *program* is prominent. For a professional meetings and events planner, the word *program* may not be pertinent, but in human resources, *program* is often used. Finding one term for all these situations would be difficult. Consequently, the terms *program* and *project* are used interchangeably. Table I.1 lists these and other terms that may be used in other contexts.

Features

Each book in the series takes a straightforward approach to make it understandable, practical, and useful. Checklists are provided, charts are included, templates are presented, and examples are explored. All are intended to show how the ROI Methodology works. The focus of these books is implementing the process and making it successful within an organization. The methodology is based on the work of hundreds of individuals who have made the ROI Methodology a successful evaluation process within their organizations.

About Pfeiffer

Pfeiffer serves the professional development and hands-on resource needs of training and human resource practitioners and gives them products to do their jobs better. We deliver proven ideas and solutions from experts in HR development and HR management, and we offer effective and customizable tools to improve workplace performance. From novice to seasoned professional, Pfeiffer is the source you can trust to make yourself and your organization more successful.

Essential Knowledge Pfeiffer produces insightful, practical, and comprehensive materials on topics that matter the most to training and HR professionals. Our Essential Knowledge resources translate the expertise of seasoned professionals into practical, how-to guidance on critical workplace issues and problems. These resources are supported by case studies, worksheets, and job aids and are frequently supplemented with CD-ROMs, Web sites, and other means of making the content easier to read, understand, and use.

Essential Tools Pfeiffer's Essential Tools resources save time and expense by offering proven, ready-to-use materials—including exercises, activities, games, instruments, and assessments—for use during a training or team-learning event. These resources are frequently offered in looseleaf or CD-ROM format to facilitate copying and customization of the material.

Pfeiffer also recognizes the remarkable power of new technologies in expanding the reach and effectiveness of training. While e-hype has often created whizbang solutions in search of a problem, we are dedicated to bringing convenience and enhancements to proven training solutions. All our e-tools comply with rigorous functionality standards. The most appropriate technology wrapped around essential content yields the perfect solution for today's on-the-go trainers and human resource professionals.

Pfeiffer *Essential resources for training and HR professionals*
www.pfeiffer.com

Isolation
of Results

Defining the Impact
of the Program

Jack J. Phillips, Ph.D.
Bruce C. Aaron, Ph.D.

Pfeiffer

A Wiley Imprint
www.pfeiffer.com

Published by Pfeiffer
An Imprint of Wiley
989 Market Street, San Francisco, CA 94103-1741
www.pfeiffer.com

Readers should be aware that Internet Web sites offered as citations and/or sources for further information may have changed or disappeared between the time this book was written and when it is read.

For additional copies/bulk purchases of this book in the U.S. please contact 800-274-4434.

Pfeiffer books and products are available through most bookstores. To contact Pfeiffer directly call our Customer Care Department within the U.S. at 800-274-4434, outside the U.S. at 317-572-3985, fax 317-572-4002, or visit www.pfeiffer.com.

Pfeiffer also publishes its books in a variety of electronic formats. Some content that appears in print may not be available in electronic books.

Library of Congress Cataloging-in-Publication Data

Phillips, Jack J., date.
  Isolation of results: defining the impact of the program/Jack J. Phillips and Bruce C. Aaron.
      p.   cm.
  Includes bibliographical references and index.
  ISBN 978-0-7879-8719-0 (pbk.)
   1. Project management.   2. Project management—Evaluation.   3. Rate of return.
I. Aaron, Bruce C.   II. Title.
  HD69.P75P488   2008
  658.4'04—dc22

                                                          2007035497

Production Editor: Michael Kay   Editorial Assistant: Julie Rodriguez
Editor: Matthew Davis   Manufacturing Supervisor: Becky Morgan
Printed in the United States of America

PB Printing 10 9 8 7 6 5 4 3 2 1

Contents

Acknowledgments from the Editors   xix

Principles of the ROI Methodology   xxi

Chapter 1: The Importance of Isolating the Effects of Programs   **1**

Challenges in Understanding a Program's Impact   2

Case Study: What Caused the Improvement?   2

Preliminary Issues in Isolating Program Effects   5

    The Need to Isolate Program Effects   6

    Chain of Impact: Initial Evidence of Program Effects   8

    Identification of Factors Other Than the Program:

        A First Step   10

Final Thoughts   12

Chapter 2: Use of Control Groups   **15**

Control Group Design   15

    Threats to Validity   15

    Basic Control Group Design   17

    Ideal Experimental Design   18

    Posttest-Only Control Group Design   20

    Which Design to Choose   21

Issues When Considering Control Groups   22

    Viability   22

    Practicality   22

Ethical Considerations   23
Potential Problems with Control Groups: A Case Example   24
Feasibility   29

Control Group Example 1: Retail Merchandise Company   31

Setting   31
Audience   32
Solution   32
Measures That Matter   32
Selection Criteria   33
Size of Groups   33
Duration of Experiment   33

Control Group Example 2: Federal Information Agency   34

Setting   34
Audience   34
Solution   35
Measures That Matter   35
Selection Criteria   35
Size of Groups   36
Duration of Experiment   36

Control Group Example 3: Midwest Electric, Inc.   36

Setting   36
Needs Assessment   37
Audience   38
Solution   39
Measures That Matter   39
Selection Criteria   39
Size of Groups   40
Duration of Experiment   40

Control Group Example 4: International Software Company   41

Setting   41
Audience   41
Solution   41
Measures That Matter   41
Selection Criteria   42

Size of Groups   42
Duration of Experiment   42
Final Thoughts   43

Chapter 3: Use of Trend Lines and Forecasts   45

Trend Lines   46
Forecasts   50
Trend Line Analysis Example 1: Micro Electronics   53
  Setting   53
  Audience   53
  Solution   53
  Measures That Matter   54
  Conditions Test   54
Trend Line Analysis Example 2: Healthcare, Inc.   54
  Setting   54
  Audience   55
  Solution   55
  Measures That Matter   56
  Conditions Test   56
Trend Line Analysis Example 3: National Book
  Company   57
  Setting   57
  Audience   57
  Solution   57
  Measures That Matter   58
  Conditions Test   58
Final Thoughts   59

Chapter 4: Use of Expert Estimates   61

Participants' Estimates of Program Impact   62
  Using Focus Groups to Obtain Participant Estimates   63
  Using Questionnaires to Obtain Participant Estimates   68
  Using Interviews to Obtain Participant Estimates   74
  Advantages and Disadvantages of Participant Estimates   75

Case Study   76
    Setting   76
    Audience   76
    Solution   77
    Measures   78
    Estimates Provided   78
    Credibility Check   78
    Methodology   79
Immediate Managers' Estimates of Program Impact   80
Senior Management's Estimates of Program Impact   82
Customers' Estimates of Program Impact   83
Experts' Estimates of Program Impact   84
Determining the Impact of Other Factors   84
Estimate Example 1: Global Financial Services   85
    Setting   85
    Audience and Solution   86
    Measures   86
    Estimates Provided   87
Estimate Example 2: Cracker Box   87
    Setting   87
    Audience and Solution   88
    Measures   88
    Estimates Provided   89
Estimate Example 3: Public Bank of Malaysia   89
    Setting   89
    Audience and Solution   89
    Measure   89
    Estimates Provided   90
Estimate Example 4: Multi-National, Inc.   90
    Setting   90
    Audience, Solution, and Measures   91
    Estimates Provided   91
The Power of Estimates   92
    Research   92
    A Demonstration   92
    Participant Reaction   93
    Management Reaction   94
    The Wisdom of Crowds   94

Key Issues in Using Estimates   95
Final Thoughts   96

Chapter 5: Use of Isolation Techniques   **99**

Matching Exercise: Isolating the Effects of
    a Program   99
Case Study: National Computer Company   102
Why Isolation Is a Key Issue   105
    Other Factors Are Always There   105
    Without It, There Is No Business Link: Evidence
        Versus Proof   105
    Other Factors and Influences Have Protective Owners   106
    To Do It Right Is Not Easy   106
    Without It, the Study Is Not Valid   106
Isolation Myths   107
Build Credibility with the Isolation Process   109
    Selecting the Technique   109
    Using Multiple Methods   110
    Building Credibility   111
Final Thoughts   112

Index   113

About the Authors   119

Acknowledgments
from the Editors

From Patti

No project, regardless of its size or scope, is completed without the help and support of others. My sincere thanks go to the staff at Pfeiffer. Their support for this project has been relentless. Matt Davis has been the greatest! It is our pleasure and privilege to work with such a professional and creative group of people.

Thanks also go to my husband, Jack. His unwavering support of my work is always evident. His idea for the series was to provide readers with a practical understanding of the various components of a comprehensive measurement and evaluation process. Thank you, Jack, for another fun opportunity!

From Jack

Many thanks go to the staff who helped make this series a reality. Lori Ditoro did an excellent job of meeting a very tight deadline and delivering a quality manuscript.

Much admiration and thanks go to Patti. She is an astute observer of the ROI Methodology, having observed and learned from hundreds of presentations, consulting assignments, and engagements. In addition, she is an excellent researcher and student of the process, studying how it is developed and how it works. She has become an ROI expert in her own right. Thanks, Patti, for your many contributions. You are a great partner, friend, and spouse.

Principles of the ROI Methodology

The ROI Methodology is a step-by-step tool for evaluating any program, project, or initiative in any organization. Figure P.1 illustrates the ROI process model, which makes a potentially complicated process simple by breaking it into sequential steps. The ROI process model provides a systematic, step-by-step approach to ROI evaluations that helps keep the process manageable, allowing users to address one issue at a time. The model also emphasizes that the ROI Methodology is a logical, systematic process that flows from one step to another and provides a way for evaluators to collect and analyze six types of data.

Applying the model consistently from one program to another is essential for successful evaluation. To aid consistent application of the model, the ROI Methodology is based on twelve Guiding Principles. These principles are necessary for a credible, conservative approach to evaluation through the different levels.

1. When conducting a higher-level evaluation, collect data at lower levels.

2. When planning a higher-level evaluation, the previous level of evaluation is not required to be comprehensive.

3. When collecting and analyzing data, use only the most credible sources.

Figure P.1. The ROI Process Model

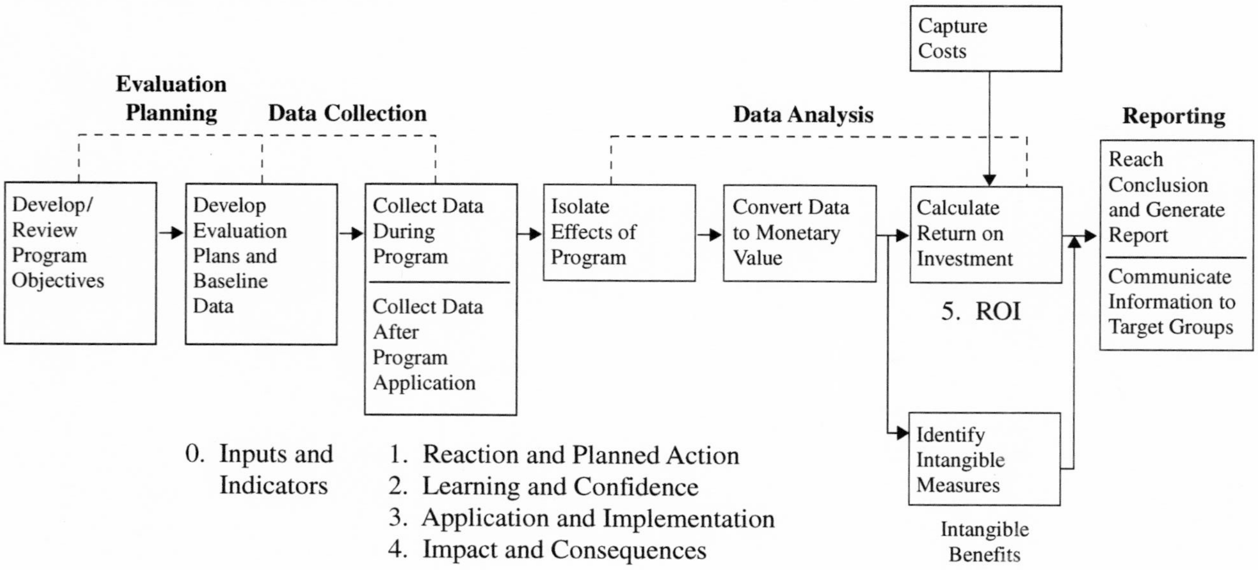

4. When analyzing data, select the most conservative alternative for calculations.

5. Use at least one method to isolate the effects of a project.

6. If no improvement data are available for a population or from a specific source, assume that little or no improvement has occurred.

7. Adjust estimates of improvement for potential errors of estimation.

8. Avoid use of extreme data items and unsupported claims when calculating ROI.

9. Use only the first year of annual benefits in ROI analysis of short-term solutions.

10. Fully load all costs of a solution, project, or program when analyzing ROI.

11. Intangible measures are defined as measures that are purposely not converted to monetary values.

12. Communicate the results of the ROI Methodology to all key stakeholders.

1

The Importance of Isolating
the Effects of Programs

The following situation is repeated often. A significant increase in performance is noted after a major program has been conducted, and the improvement appears to be linked to the program. A key manager asks, "How much of this improvement was caused by the program?" When this potentially embarrassing question is asked, it is rarely answered with any degree of accuracy or credibility. While the change in performance may be linked to the program, other factors have usually contributed to the improvement as well.

This book explores the techniques for isolating the effects of programs from other factors. These techniques are used in top organizations as they measure the return on investment of a variety of programs. This first chapter focuses on the importance of isolating the effects of a program and the challenges faced in doing so.

A cause-and-effect relationship between a program and business performance can be difficult to prove, but such a relationship can be established with an acceptable degree of accuracy. The challenge is to decide upon one or more specific techniques to isolate the effects of the program or project early in the process, usually as part of an evaluation plan. Up-front planning is the best way to ensure that appropriate techniques with minimum costs and time commitments are used.

Challenges in Understanding a Program's Impact

In organizations, initiatives unfold in complex systems of people, processes, and events. The only way to learn about the connection between a program or a project and business performance is to isolate the effects of the program on specific business measures. This step ensures that the data analysis allocates to the program only that part of the performance improvement that is actually connected with the program. If this important step is omitted, the study may be invalid because factors other than the program may have affected the outcome of the program. Factors that can affect business performance include job redesign, incentives, rewards, compensation, technology, operational systems, and other internal processes. Factors external to the targeted department, functional area, or even the organization can also influence performance. Taking full credit for performance results without accounting for other factors is unacceptable. Only the results influenced by the program should be reported to stakeholders.

Case Study: What Caused the Improvement?

The following example illustrates why isolating the effects of a program is a critical step in the evaluation process.

First Bank, a large commercial bank, had experienced a significant increase in consumer loan volume for the quarter. In an executive meeting, the chief executive officer asked the executive group why the volume had increased. The responses were interesting.

- The executive responsible for consumer lending began the discussion by pointing out that his loan officers had become more aggressive: "They have adopted an improved sales approach. They all have sales development plans in place. We are being more aggressive."

- The marketing executive added that she thought the increase was related to a new promotional program and an increase in advertising during the period. "We've had some very effective ads," she remarked.

- The chief financial officer thought the increase in loan volume was the result of falling interest rates. He pointed out that interest rates had fallen by an average of 1 percent for the last six months and added, "Each time interest rates fall, consumers borrow more money."

- The executive responsible for mergers and acquisitions felt that the change was the result of a reduction in competition: "Several competitors closed bank branches during this quarter, which had an impact on our market areas. This has driven those customers to our branches." She added, "When you have more customers, you will have more loan volume."

- The human resources vice president spoke up and said that the incentive plan for consumer loan referrals had been slightly altered, with an increase in the referral bonus for all employees who referred legitimate customers for consumer loans. This new bonus plan, in her opinion, had caused the increase in consumer loans. She concluded, "When you reward employees for bringing in customers, they will bring them in . . . in greater numbers."

- The vice president for human resources development said that a seminar on consumer lending delivered to loan officers had caused the improvement. He indicated that the seminar had been revised in order to present appropriate strategies for increasing customer prospects and was now extremely effective. He concluded, "When

you have effective training and build skills in sales, you
will increase loan volume."

These responses left the CEO wondering just what had caused
the improvement. Was it one or all of the factors? If so, how much
of the improvement was influenced by each?

Consider for just a moment: Is this situation unusual? Probably not. As is the case in many settings, the process owners
all claim credit for the improvement; yet realistically, each can
rightfully claim only a share, if any, of the actual improvement.
The challenge is to determine which isolation method would be
most appropriate. Unfortunately, because the situation has already
occurred, some of the methods for addressing this issue are not
feasible. It might be helpful to review some of the data to see
whether a time series analysis could determine the various influences and their corresponding impact. It is too late for a control
group arrangement because all parts of the bank were subject to
the various influences. It is also important to note that the people
who understand this issue best—the loan officers who are familiar with the influences—have been omitted from the meeting. Of
the many available techniques, asking the participants (the actual
performers—that is, the loan officers) to isolate the effects of a particular program or influence may be the most credible and perhaps
only way that isolation of program effects can be accomplished
in this situation. Unfortunately, in this setting, this option was
ignored.

The CEO concluded the meeting with a request for additional details from each of the participants. Unfortunately, only
one person, the chief financial officer, provided data. In his response, he said that data from the American Bankers Association indicated that when consumer loan interest rates fall, the
volume of consumer loans goes up. He applied this information
to the bank's situation to account for a large portion of the increase in loan volume. The other owners of the processes did not
respond.

We can draw some important conclusions from this case:

- Isolation of program effects must be addressed in order for any of the functions or processes designed to improve consumer loan volume to gain credibility as a source of performance improvement.

- Sometimes, the most important people in the analysis of program effects are the performers who are actually involved in the process being measured. In this case, the loan officers were most directly involved in the process of increasing loan volume and thus were in the best position to analyze which factors were influencing business performance.

- Failure to address isolation of program effects leaves a concern or even a cloud over the contribution of a particular program; doing nothing is not an option.

- The issue of isolating program effects must be addressed early in the evaluation process so that many options can be considered.

A variety of techniques are available to isolate the effects of a program. Exhibit 1.1 lists the techniques explored in this book.

The techniques can be categorized into three basic approaches: control groups, trends and forecasts, and expert estimates. These approaches can be explained in greater technical detail. A chapter is devoted to each technique, describing the approach and providing examples of its application. The methods for isolation and guidance described here are sufficiently comprehensive and accurate for practical application. They have been proven over many years, clients, and contexts.

Preliminary Issues in Isolating Program Effects

A few preliminary issues should be considered before presenting specific techniques for isolating the effects of programs. These issues

Exhibit 1.1. Techniques for Isolating the Effects of Programs and Projects

- Control group arrangement
- Trend line analysis of performance data
- Forecasting performance data
- Participant's estimate of impact
- Supervisor's estimate of impact
- Management's estimate of impact
- Estimates based on expert opinion or previous studies
- Calculation or estimation of the impact of factors other than the program
- Customer estimate of impact

further underscore the need to isolate program effects and to address the reasons for some objections to the process. This section also explores some initial steps that must be taken to make isolation of program effects an easy-to-accomplish piece of the evaluation process.

The Need to Isolate Program Effects

To many practitioners, isolating the effects of programs and projects seems logical, practical, and necessary; among others, however, it is still much debated. Some professionals argue that isolating the effects of a process (for example, training) goes against everything taught in systems thinking and team performance improvement (Brinkerhoff and Dressler, 2002). Others argue that the only way to link a program to actual business results is to isolate its effect on those business measures (Russ-Eft and Preskill, 2001).

Much of the debate centers on misunderstandings about the isolation of program effects and on the challenge of the isolation process. The first point of debate is the issue of complementary processes. It is true that many changes in processes are implemented as part of a total performance improvement initiative; as a result,

Figure 1.1. Finding a Program's Contribution

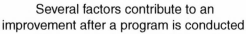

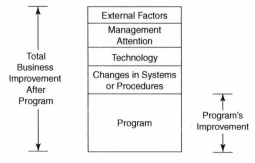

many influences work in harmony to improve business results. Often, the issue is not whether a particular process is part of the mix but how much it is needed, what specific content is appropriate, and what is the most effective method of implementation to drive its share of improvement.

The principle of isolating the effects of a program is not meant to suggest that any program should stand alone as the single variable influencing or driving significant business performance. The isolation issue comes into play, however, when different processes are influencing business results, as shown in Figure 1.1, and the different owners of the processes need information about their relative contributions. In many situations, they need to address the question "How much of the improvement was caused by the process that I am responsible for?" If they do not have a specific method for answering this question, they lose tremendous credibility, especially with the senior management team.

The second point of debate is the difficulty of isolating program effects. The classic approach—and the most credible one—is to use control group arrangements, in which one group participates in the program and another does not. However, in the majority of studies, control groups are not feasible or appropriate, so other methods must be used. Researchers sometimes use time series analysis, or forecasting. Beyond that, many researchers either give up, suggesting that isolation of program effects cannot be addressed credibly, or choose to ignore the issue, hoping that it will not be noticed by the sponsor. Neither of these responses is acceptable to a senior management team that needs to understand the link between a specific program and business success. The important point is that this issue should *always* be addressed, even if an expert estimation with an adjustment for error must be used. In this way, isolating the effects of a program becomes an essential, required step in the analysis. This requirement is the basis of Guiding Principle 5 of the ROI Methodology: Use at least one method to isolate the effects of a project.

Chain of Impact: Initial Evidence of Program Effects

Before presenting the techniques for isolating program effects, it is helpful to examine the chain of impact implied in the different levels of evaluation. As illustrated in Figure 1.2, the chain of impact must be unbroken for the program to drive business results.

Figure 1.2. The Chain of Impact

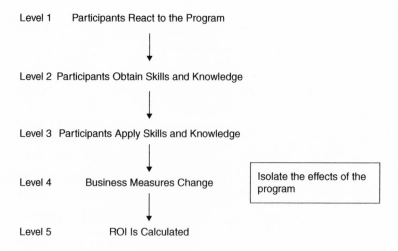

Measurable business impact achieved from a program should be derived from on-the-job application of skills and knowledge over a specified period of time after program completion. On-the-job application occurs at Level 3 of program evaluation (see Figure P.1 in "Principles of the ROI Methodology" in the front of this book; in addition, *ROI Fundamentals*, book one of this series, provides more detail on evaluation levels). Continuing with this logic, successful application of program material on the job should stem from participants learning new skills or acquiring new knowledge through the program, which is measured at Level 2. Therefore, for business results to improve (Level 4), the chain of impact implies that measurable on-the-job applications must be realized (Level 3) after new knowledge and skills are learned (Level 2). Without preliminary evidence based on the chain of impact, it would be difficult to isolate the effects of a program. If there is no learning or on-the-job application of the program material, it would be virtually impossible to conclude that the program caused any performance improvements.

This requirement for different levels of evaluation based on the chain of impact is supported in the literature (Alliger and Janak, 1989). From a practical standpoint, it means that data collection at four levels is required for an ROI evaluation. If data are collected on business results, data should also be collected at the other levels of evaluation to ensure that the program helped to produce the business results. This issue is so critical that it became the first Guiding Principle for the ROI Methodology: When a higher-level evaluation is conducted, collect data at lower levels.

This is consistent with the practices of leading organizations participating in benchmarking projects. Organizations that collect Level 4 data on business results usually report that they also collect data at the lower three levels. It is important to note, however, that the chain of impact does not prove a direct connection between a program and business results; the chain of impact is necessary but not sufficient. Taking the step to isolating the program's effects is necessary to make this connection and to pinpoint the amount of improvement caused by the program.

If the chain of impact is strong, we expect data between evaluation levels to be correlated. Several research efforts have investigated correlations between the different levels (Bledsoe, 1999; Aaron, 2005). If a significant correlation does not exist, then barriers have caused the process to break down—a logical conclusion in light of the chain of impact. However, most research in this area adds very little to the understanding of evaluation.

In different studies, correlations between two levels show varying levels of connection (or disconnection) between the two. The variation in levels of correlation doesn't mean that the concept of the levels of evaluation is flawed. Instead, as we just stated, it implies that in some cases, one or more barriers prevented a process or program from adding value. For example, most of the breakdowns occur between Level 2 and Level 3. Research has shown that as much as 90 percent of what is learned in a program is not applied and implemented (Kaufman, 2002). Even so, it is important to collect data at both levels to understand how the process of learning is working and how the system in which performers work supports the transfer of learning. A correlation analysis between levels of evaluation adds very little understanding to what must occur in practice for programs to add business value. And correlation analysis does not show a cause-and-effect relationship. Even if there is a strong correlation, the critical step of isolating the effects of a program must still be undertaken to establish a causal relationship between the program and the business improvement.

Identification of Factors Other Than the Program: A First Step

As a first step in isolating a program's impact on performance, all the key factors that may have contributed to the performance improvement should be identified. This step reveals factors other than the program that may have influenced the results, underscoring that the program is not the sole source of improvement. As a result, credit for improvement is shared among several possible variables and factors, an approach that is likely to gain the respect of management.

Several sources can potentially be used to identify major influencing variables. Sponsors, if they requested the program, may be able to identify factors that should influence the output measure. Sponsors will usually be aware of other initiatives or programs that may affect the output. Even if the program focuses on operational processes, the program sponsor or client may have insight into the other influences that may have driven performance improvement.

Direct clients as well as sponsors may also be able to provide input. The direct clients of a program are the persons who funded the initiative or provided key support for the program. These individuals are keenly interested in the issue that gave rise to the program and may be able to provide insight into other factors that may be influencing the relevant business measures. They are concerned about those measures and often understand their dynamics.

Program participants are often aware of other influences that may have caused performance improvement. After all, it is the impact of their collective efforts that is being monitored and measured. In many situations, they have witnessed previous movements in the performance measures and can pinpoint the reasons for changes. They are normally the experts on this issue.

Analysts and program developers are another potential source of information about variables that might have had an impact on results. Their needs analysis for the program would routinely have uncovered these influencing variables. In addition, program designers typically analyze such variables in addressing the issue of transfer of the skills and knowledge learned during the program.

In some situations, the participants' immediate manager may be able to identify variables that have influenced performance improvement. This is particularly useful when program participants are entry-level or low-skill employees who may not be fully aware of the variables that can influence performance.

Subject matter experts who represent different functions and processes are available. These experts have often provided input and advice needed for the program or project through all the stages of the process. They understand the dynamics of the workplace and the setting in which the program is implemented. They may be able to identify factors that are influencing the business results.

Finally, members of middle and top management may be able to identify factors other than a program that may be influencing performance, based on their experience and knowledge of the situation. Perhaps they have monitored, examined, and analyzed the other influences. Their authority within the organization often increases the credibility and acceptance of the data they provide.

Taking time to focus attention on all the variables that may have influenced performance brings additional accuracy and credibility to the program evaluation process. This step moves the process beyond the scenario in which results are presented with no mention of other influences, an omission that often destroys the credibility of an impact report. This initial step also provides a foundation for some of the techniques described in this book by identifying the variables that must be isolated in order to show the effects of a particular program.

A word of caution is appropriate here. Halting the process at this step would leave many unknowns about the actual impact of a program and might leave the client or senior management with a negative impression of the program because the analysis might have identified variables that management did not previously consider. Therefore, it is recommended that program staff members go beyond this initial step and use one or more of the techniques for isolating the impact of a program that are the focus of this book.

Final Thoughts

This brief introductory chapter has outlined the reasons why it is necessary to tackle this critical issue, isolating the effects of programs. Without it, credibility is lost, and with it, credibility is gained. That is the key issue. The next chapter focuses on the most credible method for isolating the effects of programs: using control groups.

References

Aaron, B. C. "Use the Chain of Impact to Leverage Data and Demonstrate ROI." Paper presented at the International Conference and Exposition of ASTD, Orlando, Fla., May 2005.

Alliger, G. M., and Janak, E. A. "Kirkpatrick's Levels of Training Criteria: Thirty Years Later." *Personnel Psychology,* 1989, *42,* 331–342.

Bledsoe, M. "Correlations in Kirkpatrick's Evaluation Model." Dissertation. Ann Arbor, Mich.: UMI Microform, 1999.

Brinkerhoff, R. O., and Dressler, D. "Using Evaluation to Build Organizational Performance and Learning Capability: A Strategy and a Method." *Performance Improvement,* July 2002, *41*(6), 14–21.

Kaufman, R. "Resolving the (Often-Deserved) Attacks on Training." *Performance Improvement,* July 2002, *41*(6), pp. 5–6.

Russ-Eft, D., and Preskill, H. *Evaluation in Organizations: A Systematic Approach to Enhancing Learning, Performance, and Change.* Cambridge, Mass.: Perseus, 2001.

2

Use of Control Groups

The most accurate approach to isolating the impact of a program is the use of control groups in an experimental design process (Wang, Dou, and Lee, 2002). This approach involves the use of an experimental group that participates in a specific program and a control group that does not. The composition of both groups should be as similar as possible; therefore, the selection of participants for each group should be random, if that is feasible. When random selection is used and both groups are subjected to the same environmental influences, the difference in performance of the two groups can be attributed to the program.

Control Group Design

A few variations of the control group design are briefly presented in the following sections. However, using a control group is the most credible process only if it is used appropriately. Before looking at the experimental designs, it is appropriate to discuss what factors might threaten the credibility of a control group arrangement.

Threats to Validity

When discussing the merits of various control group arrangements, it is important to address the issue of validity, which is discussed in *Data Collection*, book two of this series. Validity is the extent to which an instrument or experiment measures what it is designed to measure. Several problems may alter the measured results of a program and thus reduce the validity of an evaluation design.

The first threat involves time. Time has a way of changing things. With the passage of time, performance can improve and attitudes can change—even without the implementation of a program or project. When observing output measures of a program, always ask, "Would the same results have occurred without the program?" The control group design addresses threats to validity from events outside of a program that develop over time.

The second threat has to do with the effects of testing (also referred to as test sensitization). The experience of a test or other measurement technique might have an effect on performance or attitudes, even if no program is undertaken. Participants reflect on the pretest or other measurement, and they alter their behavior or actions toward the issue, thereby influencing the results. Studies show that simply administering pretests has substantial positive effect on performance (Wilson and Putnam, 1982).

A third threat to validity is faulty selection of the groups. A biased group might have an effect on the outcome. Naturally, some individuals will perform better than others. If a large number of overachievers or underachievers are selected for one group, the results will be distorted and atypical. This problem can be addressed by using random selection whenever feasible.

Finally, a fourth threat is mortality. Participants may drop out of the program for various reasons. If pretests and posttests are used and the number of participants in the group changes from one measurement to the other, the change makes it difficult to compare the results of the two. This difficulty is compounded by the fact that low-level performers are usually the ones who drop out of a program. The evaluation is compromised when a significant number of participants are not in the same job when the follow-up is conducted.

These challenges are the most common threats to validity, and it is essential that they be addressed when selecting the control group.

Basic Control Group Design

A basic control group design consists of an experimental group and a control group (see Figure 2.1). The experimental group participates in the program, while the control group does not. Data are gathered on both groups before and after the program. The results of the experimental group, when compared with those of the control group, reveal the impact of the program.

This design is acceptable only when the two groups are similar with respect to relevant selection criteria. The participants in each group should have approximately the same experience, ability, and working conditions, and they should be at approximately the same job level and possibly even the same location. For example, it is improper to compare frontline supervisors with middle-level managers when determining the effects of a program on results. Such a difference between groups would make it almost impossible to perform a credible analysis of post-program performance.

Figure 2.1. Control Group Design

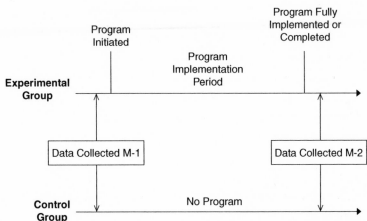

The ideal way to select control and experimental groups is on a random basis. If the participants for the two groups come from the same population and can be randomly assigned, then the evaluation design is a true control group arrangement. Random selection not only tends to equalize the groups prior to the program but also promotes a generalization of the evaluation results to other similar groups and situations. However, from a practical standpoint, selecting participants on a random basis may be difficult: for example, when time is of the essence or when an executive targets a specific group for involvement in a program. If shortcomings of the design are evident, they need to be recognized when the results are reported.

The true experimental design is one of the most powerful evaluation designs available because it combines random selection and the use of a control group. The threats to validity are controlled as tightly as possible with this design. The fact that both groups are subjected to a pretest may have an undetermined effect on performance, however. The design discussed in the next section eliminates the most common threats to validity including the influence of the pretest.

Ideal Experimental Design

Figure 2.2 shows an evaluation design that is more ideal than the classic control group design. This comprehensive design involves the use of three groups, random selection of participants, and pretesting and posttesting of two groups and posttesting only of one group. As Figure 2.2 illustrates, Group A takes a pretest, participates in the program, and takes a posttest. Group B takes a pretest and does not participate in the program but does take a posttest. Group C has no pretest, participates in the program, and does take a posttest.

The control group, Group B, isolates the time and mortality threats to validity. If measurement 1 (M-1) and measurement 2 (M-2) are equal for Group B, then it follows that neither of these

Figure 2.2. Ideal Experimental Design

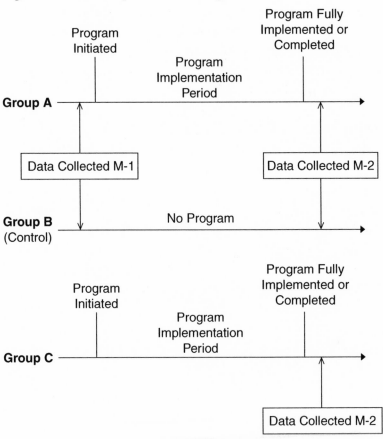

factors influenced the result. Randomization isolates the selection threat to validity. If the results for Group B are unequal, with M-2 showing a higher level of performance, then the influence of the pretest comes into play; hence the need for Group C.

Group C is used to rule out the interaction of the pretest with the effects of the program, a weakness in the classic control group design presented previously. If the posttest measurements (M-2) for Group A and Group C do not differ significantly, then the pretest had no effect on performance.

This design approaches the ultimate in experimental design. However, from a practical standpoint, obtaining three randomly selected groups may be difficult. The time, expense, inconvenience, and administrative procedures required for this arrangement may prohibit its use. Alternate designs such as the one presented in the next section can yield similar reliable results.

Posttest-Only Control Group Design

Figure 2.3 shows a more practical and less expensive alternative to the ideal experimental design: the posttest-only control group design. In this design, the randomly selected experimental and control groups are given only a posttest; neither group takes a pretest. This eliminates the effects of a pretest on the participants. Elimination of the pretest reduces the time requirement and expense of the evaluation design. In addition, this design isolates other threats to validity (Aiken, 1991).

Because of the practical nature of the posttest-only control group design, it is recommended for most studies involving measuring ROI. It is often impractical to have the three different groups that

Figure 2.3. Posttest-Only Control Group Design

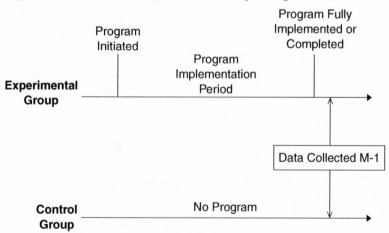

are required for the ideal experimental design. The posttest-only design is much easier to implement.

Which Design to Choose

Deciding which design you will use seems daunting at first, but answering two basic questions can help you make the decision:

1. Are you evaluating to understand whether there is a change in performance or to understand whether there is a difference in performance between groups?
2. Are data coming from people or systems?

Answering the first question tells you whether or not you need a pretest. If your program or project is intended to change a performance measure for which you have (or can get) baseline data, then understanding the difference between pre-program and post-program performance is necessary. In this case, the classic control group design is what you need. Alternatively, you may be interested only in understanding the difference in performance between two groups when one group participates in a program and another group does not. Here, pretesting is unnecessary, since the comparison is between the groups, and not within each group and then again between groups. If this is the case, then the post-program-only design can be used.

Answering the second question tells you whether there is a possibility that the pretest will influence results. If you intend to gather (with a pretest) pre-program data from people, then there is a possibility that the pretest will influence results. If you are concerned about this influence, then the ideal experimental design, using Groups A, B, and C as described earlier, should be considered. However, if you are gathering pre-program data from a system, the classic design is the approach to take, as a system is not influenced by pretests.

Issues When Considering Control Groups

Several important issues must be considered when control groups are used: viability, practicality, ethical implications, potential problems, and feasibility.

Viability

It is important for evaluators to give fair consideration to the idea of using control groups. Many take the easy way of simply not considering a control group. Thus, in a variety of settings, opportunities to benefit from the use of this isolation technique are ignored or missed because the control group arrangement was not considered. Control groups are a viable option in many organizations; however, the perception of engaging in a scientific approach makes many feel the process is impractical for them.

Practicality

Control group arrangements are used in many settings in both the private and public sectors. For example, in an impact study to measure the return on investment for a program to improve customer service, Verizon Communications used an experimental group and a control group (Keuler, 2001). The program was designed to improve feedback from Verizon's telephone customers and was expected to reduce the overall number of calls that escalated to the supervisory level. The difference between the two groups revealed the extent to which the skills were transferred to the job (Level 3) and the impact the skills were having in the workplace (Level 4). This case shows the practicality of using control groups for both Level 3 and Level 4 evaluation.

In another example, a turnover reduction program for communication specialists in a government agency used a control group and an experimental group (Phillips and Phillips, 2002). The experimental group consisted of individuals in a special program—aimed at employee retention—that allowed participants to achieve a master's degree in information science on agency time and at agency expense. The control group was carefully selected to match the experimental group in terms of job title, tenure with the agency, and college degree obtained. The differences in results between the control group and the experimental group were dramatic, showing the impact of the retention program.

Ethical Considerations

The use of control groups may convey an image that the evaluator is creating a laboratory setting, which appears to some administrators and executives to put the organization in an ethical dilemma. Concerns about purposefully withholding an opportunity from a group send up a red flag in some organizations. However, this concern can be addressed when a program is being piloted. In other words, when a decision to roll out a program to a larger group has not been made, a pilot is often offered. This offers an opportunity to select a control group from those not participating in the pilot. An example will illustrate this approach.

An international specialty manufacturing company in Malaysia developed a program for its customer service representatives, who sell directly to the public. The program was designed to improve selling skills and produce higher levels of sales. Previously, acquisition of sales skills was informal, on the job, through trial and error. The learning and development manager was convinced that formal training would significantly increase sales. Management was skeptical and wanted proof—a familiar scenario.

The program was pilot-tested by teaching sales skills to sixteen customer service representatives randomly selected from the thirty-two most recently hired. The remaining sixteen served as a control group and did not receive training. Prior to training, performance was measured, using average daily sales (sales divided by the number of days) for thirty days (or length of service, if shorter than thirty days for a specific individual), for each of the two groups. After training, the average daily sales were recorded for another thirty

days. A significant difference in the sales of the two groups occurred, and because the groups were almost identical and had been
subjected to the same environmental influences, it was concluded
that the sales difference was a result of the training program and not
other factors. In this setting, the pilot group was the experimental
group. The comparison group (control group) was easily selected.
The technique was used without the publicity and potential criti-
cism that can occur when using the control group arrangement.

Potential Problems with Control Groups: A Case Example

The control group process has some inherent problems that may
make it difficult to apply in practice. The problems that can occur
when using control groups are illustrated in the following example.

Financial Services, Inc. (FSI), is a growing financial services
company with 5,000 employees at eight hundred branch locations.
Branch offices are grouped into twelve geographic regions, each
headed by a regional manager who supervises eight district sales
managers. FSI had experienced annual turnover rates of 48 to 63
percent in the position of branch manager trainee. Although these
rates were typical of the industry, they were far too high for management, which took steps to reduce them. A needs assessment
revealed that improper selection was a key cause of the turnover.
As a result, a comprehensive selection system for branch manager
trainees was developed, including recruiting strategies, interviewing
guidelines, evaluation guidelines, and individual feedback. After
the elements were developed, district sales managers implemented
the selection system procedures and were taught how to train their
branch managers in the program's concepts.

To measure the impact of the program, a control group arrangement was used. The program was implemented on an experimental
basis in one-third of the company's branches. The other two-thirds
of the branches served as a control group. During the six months
after the program was implemented, significant differences were reported between the program group and the control group. After the

six months, when the measurement was to take place, elements of the system had begun to be used in parts of the control group, diluting the purity of the control group for comparison purposes. The program had been so successful in the program group that managers in the rest of the company asked for it to be implemented in their regions and districts.

This scenario reveals several problems that can quickly be identified:

- The selection criteria for the groups are not clear. Having one-third of the branches in the experimental group and two-thirds in the control group suggests that the selection process was far from random and criteria were ill-defined. Specific selection criteria should result in groups that are as similar as possible.

- The groups were much too large, losing their experimental characteristics. Usually, experimental groups involve a small number of people because the project is an experiment. Also, if possible, each group should be of equal size, to facilitate comparison between the two groups.

- The program was much too long. The duration of a program must strike a delicate balance; the program should be long enough for a trend or pattern to emerge in the two groups, yet not so long that contamination occurs.

- Contamination is perhaps the most serious problem. The success identified in the experimental group quickly influenced the control group. This contamination was practically encouraged by the experimental design. District sales managers were prepared for the process but were asked to implement it in only a few locations, withholding the solution from the branches that were part of the control group. This arrangement invited contamination; the managers in the control group quickly began to use the new process when they realized it was working.

- Perhaps a control group was the wrong isolation technique for this situation. If this was indeed the solution that was needed for an expensive problem, was it prudent to wait almost a year to implement it in two-thirds of the organization? The answer is probably no.

Let's look more closely at some of the problems that can occur when using control groups.

The first major problem is that the control group process is inappropriate for many situations. For some types of programs, it is not a good idea to withhold the program from one group while providing it to another. This is particularly important in programs involving critical skills, processes, or technologies that are needed immediately on the job. For example, in entry-level training, employees need basic skills to perform their jobs. It would be inappropriate to withhold training from a group of new employees so that this group can be compared with a group that receives the training. Although this would reveal the impact of initial training, it would be devastating to the individuals who are struggling to learn necessary skills and trying to cope with a new job situation. In the previous example of the Malaysian company, a control group was feasible because the program was not essential to the job and the organization was not completely convinced that it would add value in terms of increasing sales.

This barrier keeps many control groups from being implemented. Often, management is not willing to withhold a process from one area to see how it works in another. However, in practice, a control group arrangement often develops naturally when a program is implemented throughout an organization. If it will take several months for everyone in the organization to participate in a program, there may be enough time for a comparison between the initial group involved and the last group involved. In these cases, it is critical to ensure that the groups are matched as closely as possible so that the first two groups are very similar to the last two groups. The challenge is to address this issue early enough to influence the implementation schedule so that similar groups can be used in the comparison.

The second problem that occurs in control group arrangements involves selection of the groups. From a practical perspective, having identical control and experimental groups is virtually impossible. Dozens of factors can affect employee performance; some of them are individually matched, and others are contextual. When the output can be influenced by as many as forty or fifty factors, considering all the factors is almost impossible, especially if a large number of groups is involved. Using the Pareto principle (20 percent of the variables will influence 80 percent of the outcome) makes the challenge of selecting groups manageable. Take a realistic approach, and address a reasonable number of factors. In practical terms, it is best to select group members on the basis of the three to five variables that would most influence their performance (like number of years on the job, job classification, and score on a written pretest). Ideally, the values of the chosen variables should be exactly the same in each group. Practically, the values of the chosen variables should be as similar as possible within each group. In summary, practical use of control groups must take into consideration the constraints of a work setting and focus on the most critical influences on the output measure (besides the program).

A third potential problem with control group arrangements is contamination, which occurs when participants in the program influence individuals in the control group. Sometimes, members of the control group will observe changes in the behavior of those in the experimental group and model those behaviors, with no consideration of why the behavior has changed. At other times, participants in the control group come to the realization that a program is being implemented to which they have not been invited, thus influencing their behavior. In either case, the experiment becomes contaminated because the influence of the program filters to the control group. Contamination can be minimized by ensuring that control groups and experimental groups are at different locations, have different shifts, or are on different floors in the same building. When this is not possible, it is sometimes helpful to explain to both groups that one group will participate in the program now and another will participate at a later date. Also, it may be helpful to appeal to the sense of responsibility of those involved in the program and ask them not to share the information with others.

Closely related to the problem of contamination is the issue of duration of the control group arrangement. The longer a control group and experimental group comparison operates, the greater the likelihood that influences other than the program will affect the results. More factors will enter into the situation, contaminating the results. Nevertheless, enough time must pass to allow a clear pattern of the relationship between the two groups to emerge. As mentioned earlier, the timing of control group comparisons must strike a delicate balance, waiting long enough for their performance differences to show but not so long that the results become seriously contaminated.

A fifth problem occurs when the different groups function under different environmental influences. If the groups are in different locations, their environmental influences may be different. Sometimes, the way in which the groups are selected can help prevent this problem. Another tactic is to use more groups than necessary and then discard the results from those that turn out to have some environmental discrepancies.

A sixth problem with using control groups is that it may appear too research oriented for many business organizations. For example, management may not want to take the time to experiment before proceeding with a program or may not want to withhold an experimental program from a group just to measure program impact. Because of this concern, some evaluators do not entertain the idea of using control groups. When the process is used, however, some organizations conduct it with pilot participants as the experimental group and nonparticipants as the control group. Under this arrangement, members of the control group are not informed of their control group status.

Because the use of a control group arrangement is an effective technique for isolating the impact of programs, it should be considered as a strategy when a major ROI evaluation is planned. In such situations, it is important for the program impact to be isolated with a high level of accuracy; the primary advantage of the control group process is accuracy. About one-third of the more than two hundred published studies on the ROI Methodology use the control group process.

Feasibility

Several issues must be thought through before use of a control group can be considered feasible. Every attempt should be made to use this technique because it is the most credible process. Here are a few questions to help determine whether a control group arrangement is a feasible isolation technique for a program:

- Is the population large enough to divide into groups?

- Is the population homogeneous—that is, does it represent similar jobs and similar environments?

- What is the particular measure that matters to the organization?

- What variables may be affecting the measure? These variables would be used to select the comparison groups for the control group arrangement.

- Which of the variables most strongly influences the output measure (or measures)?

- Can the program be withheld from a particular group? Sometimes, this situation occurs naturally because it takes a long time to roll out a program. Employees who participate in the program last may be three to six months behind those who participate in the program first, creating an opportunity to compare the last group with the first group.

- Is a pilot offering planned, and could the pilot group be selected to facilitate comparison with other nonparticipating groups?

When the control group arrangement is selected as a viable and feasible process, several rules are helpful.

- Keep the groups separated in different locations, different buildings, different shifts, or different floors.

- Minimize communication between the groups.

- Do not let members of the control group or the experimental group know that they are part of an experiment and are being compared with others.

- Monitor data on a short-term basis, to check for improvements in both groups.

- Try to prevent the Hawthorne effect (improvement that results from the fact of being observed) in the experimental group. Other than that required by the program design, the amount of attention paid to the group should be normal.

- Minimize the effect of the self-fulfilling prophecy by not creating expectations beyond the norm that may

influence the results. For example, do not tell people
that they are part of a special group and that top
performance is expected.

The control group arrangement is a powerful method and can
be made practical. The next few sections consist of case studies that
detail how control groups have been decided on and structured in
real situations.

Control Group Example 1:
Retail Merchandise Company

Setting

Retail Merchandise Company (RMC) is a national chain of 420
stores, located in most major U.S. markets. RMC sells small household items, gifts of all types, electronics, jewelry, and personal acces-
sories. It does not sell clothes or major appliances. RMC executives
had been concerned about slow sales growth and were experiment-
ing with several programs designed to boost sales. One concern
focused on interaction with customers. Sales associates were not
actively involved in the sales process; they usually waited for a
customer to make a purchasing decision and then processed the
sale. Several store managers had analyzed the situation to determine whether more communication with customers would boost
sales. The analysis revealed that the use of very simple techniques
to probe for a customer's needs and then guide the customer to a
purchase should boost sales in each store.

The senior executives asked the learning and development staff
to experiment with a simple program to teach customer interaction
skills to a small group of sales associates. A program produced
by an external supplier was chosen in order to avoid the cost of
development, in case the program proved ineffective. The specific
charge from the management team was to implement the program
in three stores, monitor the results, and make recommendations.

If the program increased sales and provided a significant payoff for RMC, it would be implemented in other stores.

Audience

The participants (sales associates) were typical of retail store employees. Few (if any) were college graduates, and most had only a few months of retail store experience. They were not considered professional employees but rather were seen as clerical and administrative workers. Historically, they had not been involved in discussing sales with customers except in the course of processing transactions. This program was designed to shift that paradigm so that sales associates would be more actively involved in the sales experience.

Solution

The needs analysis determined that the sales staff did not have the skills necessary to be engaged with customers. Therefore, the learning and development staff decided to implement a program called Interactive Selling Skills, which used frequent skill practice to help participants learn the required knowledge and skills and then reinforce the knowledge gained during the program. The program consisted of two days of training, during which participants had an opportunity for skill practice with a fellow classmate. The training was followed by three weeks of on-the-job application. The third and final day of the program included a discussion of problems, issues, barriers, and concerns in regard to the use of the new skills. Additional practice and fine tuning of the skills were also part of this final session. The program, an existing product from an external supplier, was applied in the electronics area of three stores. The program was taught by members of the supplier's staff for a predetermined facilitation fee.

Measures That Matter

The specific measure undergoing analysis was the average weekly sales per associate. These data, by store and by individual, were readily available from each store's sales receipts records. A history of sales data was also available.

Selection Criteria

Although many different factors could influence sales, after discussion with several store executives, four criteria were selected. Stores were selected based on similarities in

- *Previous store performance*. Weekly sales per associate for a six-month period.

- *Sales volume*. Annual sales volume for the store.

- *Traffic flow*. For security purposes, customers were routinely monitored as they came in and out of the store. This monitoring recorded the traffic flow.

- *Market*. The average household disposable income in each area was available in the company's marketing database and was one of the key measures that influenced the selection of each store.

These four factors were used to select two matching groups. (Three stores received the training; three stores did not.) These factors were selected because they influenced sales more than any other factors.

Size of Groups

There were sixteen associates in each of the six stores, providing two equal-sized groups: forty-eight in the experimental group and forty-eight in the control group. This would be enough participants to see whether differences between the groups occurred, yet would not be too expensive.

Duration of Experiment

The experiment ran for three months. The evaluation team thought that would be long enough to allow the team to see the impact of such simple skills on sales. During the three months, participants would have ample opportunity to use the new skills in a variety of situations and with a significant number of customers.

For the rest of the story of RMC, see *Proving the Value of HR: ROI Case Studies*, by Patricia Pulliam Phillips and Jack J. Phillips, published by the ROI Institute.

Control Group Example 2: Federal Information Agency

Setting

The Federal Information Agency (FIA) collects and distributes many types of important and sensitive information to a variety of stakeholders. FIA was experiencing an unacceptable rate of employee turnover among a group of communication specialists—averaging 38 percent in the preceding year alone. The high turnover was placing a strain on the agency's ability to recruit trained replacements. An analysis of exit interviews revealed that employees were leaving for jobs with higher salaries. Because FIA was somewhat limited in its ability to provide competitive salaries, it was having difficulty competing with the private sector. Although salary increases and adjustments in pay would be necessary to avoid turnover, FIA was also exploring other options. The annual employee survey indicated that employees were very interested in attending an on-site master's degree program on agency time.

Audience

The individuals targeted were 1,500 communications specialists who had degrees in various fields: communications, computer science, and electrical engineering. Only a few had master's degrees in their specialty. Among these 1,500, roughly a third were considered high-potential employees who were destined for leadership assignments in the organization. The others were needed for continuing work in their assigned positions.

Solution

The solution was an in-house master's degree program offered by a regional state university. The program would be presented at no cost to the participating employees and conducted during normal work hours. Both morning and afternoon classes were available, each representing three hours of class time per week. Participants were allowed to take one or two courses per semester (and one course during the summer session) but were discouraged from taking more than two courses per term. On this schedule, the program could be completed in three years.

Measures That Matter

The measure that was monitored was the voluntary employee turnover rate, measured monthly. Of particular interest were employees in the first four years of employment. The records showed that once individuals had been employed for four years, they would usually continue for a longer period of time, and the turnover rate went down considerably.

Selection Criteria

The experimental group consisted of participants in the program, and a matching control group was selected, using three criteria, although many factors could affect an employee's decision to leave. The criteria deemed most important and used to match control group participants to participants in the graduate program were

- · Possession of an undergraduate (B.S.) degree

- Job status (for example, job title and pay grade)

- Tenure with the agency

Size of Groups

One hundred individuals were selected for the program, and one hundred matching control group members were selected. The individuals not in the program were selected to match those in the program group in regard to the three criteria identified earlier.

Duration of Experiment

The experiment ran for four years—three years to take the first group through the program and one year post-program to continue to measure turnover.

For more details on the FIA case, see *Proving the Value of HR* (Phillips and Phillips, 2007).

Control Group Example 3: Midwest Electric, Inc.

Setting

Midwest Electric, Inc. (MEI) is a growing electric utility that serves several midwestern states. Since deregulation of the industry, MEI has been on a course of diversification and growth. Through a series of acquisitions, MEI has moved outside its traditional operating areas into several related businesses. MEI experienced significant workplace changes as it transformed from a bureaucratic, sluggish organization into a lean, competitive force in the marketplace. These changes placed tremendous pressure on employees to develop multiple skills and perform additional work. Employees, working in teams, had to constantly strive to reduce costs, maintain excellent quality, boost productivity, and generate new and efficient ways to supply customers and improve service.

Like many companies in industries in a deregulated environment, MEI has detected symptoms of employee stress. The company's safety and health department suggested that employee stress could be lowering productivity and reducing employee effectiveness. Stress was also considered a significant risk to employee health. Research has shown that high levels of stress are commonplace in many work groups and that organizations are taking steps to help employees and work groups reduce stress in a variety of ways. The vice president of human resources asked the training and education department, with the help of the safety and health department, to develop a program for work groups to help them alleviate stressful situations and deal more productively and effectively with job-induced stress.

Needs Assessment

Because it was a large organization with sophisticated human resources systems, MEI had an extensive database on employee-related measures. MEI took pride in being one of the leaders in human resources practices in its industry. Needs assessments were routinely conducted, and the human resources vice president was willing to allow sufficient time for an adequate needs assessment before proceeding with the program.

The overall purpose of the needs assessment was to identify the causes of a perceived problem. The needs assessment would

- Confirm that a problem with stress existed and assess the actual impact of this problem

- Uncover potential causes of the problem within work units, the company, and the work environment, and provide insight into potential remedies

Sources of data for the needs assessment included company records, external research, team members, team leaders, and managers. The assessment began with a review of external research that identified the factors usually related to high stress and the consequences of high stress in work groups. The consequences led to identification of relevant business measures that could be monitored at MEI.

The external research then led to a review of several key data items in company records, including attitude surveys, medical claims, Employee Assistance Plan records, safety and health records, and exit interview transcripts. Attitude survey results from the previous year were reviewed for low scores on the specific questions that could yield stress-related symptoms. Medical claims were analyzed by codes to identify the extent of those related to stress-induced illnesses. Employee Assistance Plan data were reviewed to determine the extent to which employees were using the provisions and services of the plan that were perceived to be stress-related. Safety records were reviewed to determine whether specific accidents were stress-related or whether causes of accidents could be traced to high levels of stress. In each of the preceding areas, current data were compared with data from the previous year to determine whether stress-related measures had changed. In addition, data were compared against expected norms found through the external research, where available. Finally, exit interviews from the previous six months were analyzed to determine the extent to which stress-related situations were factors in employees' decisions to voluntarily leave MEI.

A small sample of employees (ten team members) was interviewed in order to discuss their work-life situation and uncover symptoms of stress at work. A small group of managers (five) was interviewed with the same purpose. To provide more detail, a 10 percent sample of employees received a questionnaire that explored the same issues. MEI has 22,550 employees, including 18,220 nonsupervisory team members.

Audience

The audience for this program was members of intact work teams who voluntarily enrolled in the program to reduce stress. These teams had to be experiencing high levels of stress and be willing to participate in a program of planned stress reduction.

Solution

The program, Stress Management for Intact Work Teams, involved several activities occurring in ten sessions. Initially, the entire group completed the comprehensive self-assessment tool called StressMap® so that group members could see where they stood on a scale of twenty-one stress factors. Then a three- to four-hour StressMap debriefing session helped individuals interpret their scores. This was followed by a four-hour module suited to the needs of the group. All this was done in one day. Approximately three to four hours of telephone follow-up was included in the process.

Measures That Matter

This program focused on multiple measures:

- Unplanned and unexpected absenteeism

- Voluntary turnover

- Reported monthly health care costs for employees

- Reported monthly safety costs for employees

Selection Criteria

Six pairs of intact teams were selected. Each pair consisted of a program group and a matching control group. Several criteria were used in selecting the control group:

- The control group and its corresponding program group had to have the same types of performance measures in their operating group. At least 75 percent of the measures had to be common between the two groups.

This action provided an opportunity to compare the performance of the groups in the six months preceding the program.

- Each control group and corresponding experimental group had to have the same function code. (At MEI, all work groups were assigned a function code that indicated the type of work they performed, such as finance and accounting, engineering, or plant operations.)

- Group size was also a factor. The number of employees in the control group and the number in the corresponding program group had to be within 20 percent of each other.

- Average tenure was also used as a selection criterion. The average tenures of employees in the two groups in a pair had to be within two years of each other. At MEI, as at many other utilities, average tenure was high.

Size of Groups

The six pairs of groups represented a total of 138 team members in the experimental groups and 132 team members and six managers in the control groups.

Duration of Experiment

Data on all four measures were reviewed after six months; the results were then extrapolated for a complete year to determine an annual impact.

More details on the MEI case can be found in *Proving the Value of HR* (Phillips and Phillips, 2007).

Control Group Example 4: International Software Company

Setting

International Software Company (ISC) produces payroll software for companies with a small number of employees. Several enhancements can be purchased to perform other routines involving employee statistics and data. In some cases, the data are relevant to staffing and manpower-planning issues. The company has a customer database of over 1,500 users. For the most part, the customers use only the payroll functions of the software.

Each year, ISC hosts a conference during which users discuss issues they have encountered during implementation; new uses of the software; and how the software could be adjusted, modified, or enhanced to add value to their organizations. The conference is also an opportunity for ISC to get referrals and sell enhanced versions of its software.

Audience

The audience for this project was the individuals who attended the users' conference. To attend the conference, they must have purchased the software and used it primarily for the payroll option.

Solution

The solution was a two-day conference designed to improve customer satisfaction with the software, upgrade software users to other options, and obtain referrals to potential clients. There was no charge for attendance; however, the participants had to pay for their own travel arrangements and hotel accommodations.

Measures That Matter

Several measures were monitored in the control group arrangement to ensure the success of this program:

- Sales of upgrades to current customers (sales to existing clients)

- Referrals to new clients

- Increase in customer satisfaction as measured on the annual satisfaction survey

Selection Criteria

Four criteria were used to select individuals for the comparison groups. The conference attendees became the experimental group, and a comparison group of users that did not attend the conference became the control group. The two groups were matched using the following criteria:

- *Type of organization.* Type of business, according to standard industrial classification

- *Extent of use.* The extent to which a customer used the upgraded software options beyond the basic payroll processing

- *Sales.* Sales volume to date, which reflected the number of employees in the client business

- *Longevity.* Longevity of the customer, measured in years of using the current software

Size of Groups

There were 124 users at the conference, and a matching control group of 121 was selected, using the criteria just outlined.

Duration of Experiment

The experiment lasted for one year and tracked the three selected measures, sales, referrals, and customer satisfaction, in order to compare the data from conference participants in the year after the program with the data from users who did not attend the conference. For example, the average number of referrals that came through the conference was compared with the number of referrals from other channels. In addition, the number of upgrades made by users who attended the conference was compared with the number of upgrades made by those who did not attend. Finally, the customer satisfaction data were compared for the two groups.

Final Thoughts

This chapter has explored the most powerful technique for isolating the effects of a program: the classic comparison of performance in an experimental group and a control group. Three designs were introduced in this chapter: the classic design, the ideal design, and the post-program-only design. Each design is useful depending on the needs of the evaluation. Although there are issues concerning the use of control and experimental comparisons, including viability, feasibility, and ethical implications, as shown in the case studies, these comparisons can be made when the conditions warrant.

Due to practical considerations, however, the use of control and experimental groups is at times not feasible in organizational settings, and thus other approaches have to be explored in order to address the issue of isolating the effects of a program on performance. The trade-off often pits research principles against feasibility. In reality, most of the decisions made by management are not based on valid and reliable data. Instead, they are often made on management's intuitive assessment of the data presented to it. In recent years, progress has been made in developing innovative approaches to isolate the effects of a program on output performance, using data appropriate to management needs. The next chapter focuses on such an approach: trends and forecasts.

References

Aiken, L. *Psychological Testing and Assessment*. (7th ed.) Boston: Allyn & Bacon, 1991.

Keuler, D. "Measuring ROI for Telephonic Customer Service Skills." In P. P. Phillips (ed.), *In Action: Measuring Return on Investment*, Vol. 3. Alexandria, Va.: ASTD, 2001.

Phillips, P. P., and Phillips, J. J. "Evaluating the Impact of a Graduate Program in a Federal Agency." In P. P. Phillips (ed.), *In Action: Measuring ROI in the Public Sector*. Alexandria, Va.: ASTD, 2002.

Phillips, P. P., and Phillips, J. J. *Proving the Value of HR: ROI Case Studies*. Birmingham, Ala.: ROI Institute, 2007.

Wang, G., Dou, Z., and Lee, N. "A Systems Approach to Measuring Return on Investment (ROI) for HRD Interventions." *Human Resource Development Quarterly*, 2002, *13*(2), 203–224.

Wilson, V. L., and Putnam, R. R. "A Metanalysis of Pretest Sensitization Effects in Experimental Design." *American Education Research Journal*, 1982, *19*, 249–258.

3

Use of Trend Lines and Forecasts

W hen a control group analysis is not feasible for isolating the impact of a program, the next logical choice is some type of time series analysis. This chapter describes two closely related techniques. Trend line analysis is a simple process of using pre-program data to forecast the value of a measure at some future point. The actual value of the performance measure after program implementation is compared with the projected trend value, and the difference in performance is attributed to the program. Trend line analysis can be used only when no influences other than the program have affected the measure.

The forecast method is a more general technique that is used when influences outside of a program have entered the process. A mathematical relationship is developed to take the outside influences into account so that the value of a measure can be forecast rather than just projected on a trend line. The forecast measure is compared with the actual measure after program implementation in order to show the program's contribution. The analytical tools involved in these forecasting techniques are fairly simple; nonetheless, forecasting can sometimes become complicated, as will be discussed later in this chapter.

This chapter has good news and bad news. The good news is that the techniques of trend line analysis and forecasting are credible processes that can accurately isolate the effects of programs.

The bad news is that they work less than 25 percent of the time because workplaces are so dynamic and because the mathematical relationships between the variables are often not present in the real world. However, because these methods are relatively easy to use, it is worthwhile for evaluators to pursue them in order to isolate the effects of programs.

Trend Lines

Trend line analysis is a useful technique for approximating the impact of a program. A trend line is drawn, using previous performance as a base and extending the trend into the future. After the program is conducted, actual performance is compared with the projected value, the trend line. Any improvement in performance over what the trend line predicted can then be reasonably attributed to the program, if two conditions are met:

1. The trend prior to the program would have been expected to continue if the program had not been implemented to alter it. Ask this question: "If the program had not been implemented, would this trend have continued on the path that was established before the program was initiated?" The process owner (or owners) should be able to provide input to help answer this question. If the answer is no, trend line analysis will not be used. If the answer is yes, the second condition must still be met.

2. No other new variables or influences entered the process after the program was conducted. The key word is *new*; the trend was established as a result of the influences already in place. Ask this question: "Have influences other than the program entered the process?" If the answer is yes, another method must be used. If the answer is no, the trend line analysis will result in a reasonable and credible estimate of the impact of the program.

Figure 3.1. Trend Line Analysis of Sales

Figure 3.1 shows the trend line analysis of sales revenue in a retail store chain. The figure presents data from before and after a sales incentive program was introduced in July. The data showed an upward trend prior to implementation of the incentive program. Although the program had a dramatic effect on sales, the trend line shows that some improvement would have occurred anyway, according to the previously established trend. It is tempting to measure the improvement by comparing the average of the six months of sales prior to the program ($37.6 million) with the average of the six months of sales after the program ($44.1 million), yielding a $6.5 million difference. However, it would be more accurate to estimate the program's impact by comparing the six-month average after the program with the trend line average that was projected for the same period ($42.1 million), a difference of $2 million. Using this more conservative estimate increases the accuracy and credibility of the isolation process. In this case, the two conditions outlined earlier were met (the answer was yes on the first question and no on the second question). As a result, the $2 million improvement in sales can reasonably be attributed to the program.

Pre-program data must be available in order for trend line analysis to be used, and the data should have a reasonable degree of stability. If the variance of the data is high, the stability of the trend line becomes an issue. If this is an extremely critical issue and the stability cannot be assessed from a direct plot of the data, more detailed statistical analyses can be used to determine whether the data are stable enough to make the projection (Salkind, 2000).

A trend line projected directly from the historical data by means of graphics software may be acceptable. If additional accuracy is needed, the trend line can be projected by using a simple analytical routine available in many calculators and software packages—for example, Microsoft Excel.

The use of trend line analysis becomes more dramatic and convincing when a measure that was moving in an undesirable direction is completely turned around as a result of a program. For example, Figure 3.2 shows a trend line analysis of voluntary employee turnover in a large hotel chain. As the figure shows, turnover was increasing, moving in an undesirable direction. The retention program turned the situation around so that the actual results were in the other direction: turnover data showed a decreasing trend. The trend line process highlights dramatic improvement. In Figure 3.2, the trend line's projected value for turnover is significantly higher than the actual results.

Figure 3.2. Trend Line Analysis of Voluntary Turnover of Hotel Staff

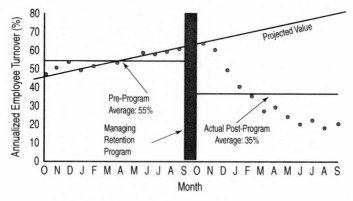

A primary disadvantage of the trend line approach is that it is not always accurate. Use of this approach assumes that the factors that influenced the performance measure prior to the program are still in place after the program, except for the implementation of the program (in other words, that the trends established prior to the program continue in the same direction). Also, trend line analysis assumes that no new influences affected the situation when the program was conducted or subsequently. This is not always the case.

The primary advantage of trend line analysis is that it is simple and inexpensive. If historical data are available, a trend line can quickly be drawn and differences estimated. While trend line analysis is not exact, it does provide a very quick assessment of a program's impact. About 15 percent of the more than two hundred published studies on the ROI Methodology use trend line analysis. However, when variables other than the program being analyzed enter the situation, additional analysis is needed.

Trend line analysis is often easy to perform, and it can yield a credible estimate of a program's impact. To use trend lines effectively, you must be able to answer yes to each of these four questions:

1. Are historical data available for the measure at hand?
2. Are at least six data points available?
3. Do the historical data appear to be stable when they are plotted over time?
4. Do you anticipate that no other new influences, factors, or processes will come into play or be implemented at the same time as the program?

In conclusion, here are some general guidelines for working with trend line analysis:

1. Use pre-program data to draw the trend line for your chosen measure.

2. Trend lines are easily developed in Microsoft Excel. Input the data in columns, then use the chart wizard to create the graph.

3. In addition to drawing the trend line, check with the process owners about whether a trend had begun before the onset of the program. Ask whether the trend probably would have continued during the post-analysis period if the program had not been implemented. If the answer to this question is no, trend line analysis cannot be used for the measure under consideration.

4. After the program has been implemented, ask whether any additional factors entered the process during the evaluation time period. If other factors likely influenced the measure being tracked, trend line analysis cannot be used for the measure under consideration.

5. If the question in item 3 is answered yes and the question in item 4 is answered no, trend line analysis is a credible way of isolating the effects of your program.

Forecasts

A more analytical approach to trend line analysis is the use of forecasting methods that can predict changes in performance measures based on variables other than the program under analysis. This approach represents a mathematical interpretation of the trend line analysis discussed earlier when additional new variables have entered the situation at the time of program implementation. The basic premise is that the actual performance of a measure (which is related to the program) will be compared with the forecast value of that measure (which is based on the other influences). A linear model, in the form $y = ax + b$, is appropriate when only one other variable influences the output performance and that relationship is characterized by a straight line. Instead of drawing the straight line, a linear equation is developed, which calculates a value for the anticipated performance improvement.

An example will help to explain the application of this process. A large retail store chain with a strong sales culture implemented a sales training program for sales associates. The three-day program was designed to enhance sales skills and prospecting techniques. It was assumed that application of the skills taught in the program would increase the sales volume for each associate. An important measure of the program's success was the sales per employee six months after the program compared with the same measure prior to the program. Prior to the program, the average daily sales per employee, using a one-month average, were $1,100 (rounded to the nearest $100). Six months after the program, the average daily sales per employee were $1,500 (average for the sixth month). Both of these sales numbers are average values for a specific group of participants. Two related questions must be answered: (1) Is the difference in the two values attributable to the training program? (2) Did other factors influence the post-program sales level?

A review of potential influencing factors with several store executives found that only one factor, the level of advertising, appeared to have changed significantly during the period under consideration. A review of previous data on sales per employee and levels of advertising revealed a direct relationship between the two. As expected, when advertising expenditures were increased, sales per employee increased proportionately.

The advertising staff had developed a mathematical relationship between advertising and sales. Using the historical values, a simple linear model yielded the following relationship: $y = 140 + 40x$, where y is the daily sales per employee and x is the level of advertising expenditures per week divided by 1,000. This equation was developed by the marketing department, using the method of least squares to derive a mathematical relationship between two columns of data (advertising and sales). The least squares function is a routine option on some calculators and is included in many software packages. Figure 3.3 shows the linear relationship between

Figure 3.3. Relationship Between Advertising and Daily Sales

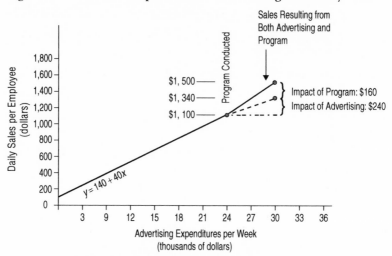

advertising and sales. It is important to remember that this relationship had already been developed by the advertising department.

The level of weekly advertising expenditures in the month preceding the program was $24,000, and the level of expenditures in the sixth month after the program was $30,000. Assuming that the other factors influencing sales were insignificant, store executives determined the impact of the advertising by plugging in the new advertising expenditure amount (30) for x and calculating the daily sales, which yielded $1,340. Therefore, the new sales level caused by the increase in advertising was $1,340, as shown in Figure 3.3. Because the actual sales value was $1,500, $160 ($1,500 – $1,340) must be attributed to the program. The effects of both the program and advertising are shown in Figure 3.3.

A major disadvantage of this forecasting approach occurs when several variables enter the process. The complexity multiplies, and use of sophisticated statistical packages for multiple variable analyses becomes necessary. Even then, a good fit of the data to the model may not be possible. Unfortunately, some organizations have not developed mathematical relationships for output variables as a function of one or more inputs. Without them, the forecasting method is difficult to use.

The primary advantage of this forecasting process is that it can accurately predict business performance measures without the program, if appropriate data and models are available. The use of more complex models is an option for practitioners familiar with the assumptions and requirements of general linear model techniques. The presentation of more complex methods is beyond the scope of this book and is contained in other publications (see, for example, Armstrong, 2001).

Approximately 5 percent of the published studies on the ROI Methodology use this forecasting technique.

Trend Line Analysis Example 1: Micro Electronics

Setting

A series of programs was conducted as part of an improvement effort for Micro Electronics, a manufacturer of electronics components. One measure of quality was the reject rate—the percentage of items returned for rework. Because of an overall emphasis on quality in the preceding year, there had been a downward trend in the reject rate. However, the movement had been gradual, and there was still room for improvement.

Audience

In one work unit, a continuous process improvement program was implemented in order to improve the reject rate. All twenty-six employees in the process unit were involved in the program.

Solution

The solution was a continuous process improvement program, conducted two hours per day over a one-week period. During this program, employees examined each of the process variables in the work unit and discussed and brainstormed ways to make improvements. The result was improvement in several of the processes, which addressed the measure in question—the reject rate.

Figure 3.4. Reject Rate

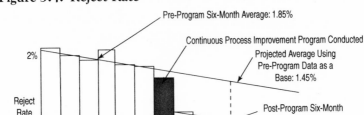

Pre-Program Six-Month Average: 1.85%

Continuous Process Improvement Program Conducted

Projected Average Using Pre-Program Data as a Base: 1.45%

Post-Program Six-Month Average: 0.7%

2%

Reject Rate

J F M A M J J A S O N D J

Month

Measures That Matter

The measure of interest was the reject rate in the work unit, which had been as high as 2 percent at times. The goal was to get the reject rate as close to zero as possible. Figure 3.4 shows a plot of the data.

Conditions Test

The employees, the quality control staff, and the team leader knew of no influences other than those from the program that entered into the process during the evaluation period. They also concluded that the downward trend would most likely have continued—at least for the six months during the evaluation period. With these two conditions met, it is possible to attribute the difference between 1.45 percent and 0.7 percent—a 0.75 percent decrease in the reject rate—to the process improvement program.

Trend Line Analysis Example 2: Healthcare, Inc.

Setting

Healthcare, Inc. (HI), provides a variety of health care services through a chain of hospitals, health maintenance organizations, and clinics. HI, a regional provider, has grown steadily in the last few years and has earned a reputation as a progressive and financially sound company. HI is publicly owned, and its aggressive management team is poised for additional growth.

Sexual harassment is a significant employee relations issue in the United States. Sexual harassment claims in the health care industry and throughout the nation continue to increase, sparked in part by increased public awareness of the issue and victims' increased willingness to report harassment. HI had experienced an increasing number of sexual harassment complaints, and a significant number of them resulted in legal charges and lawsuits. Executives found the complaint record excessive and a persistent and irritating problem. In addition, HI was experiencing an unusually high level of turnover, part of which might have been linked to sexual harassment.

Audience

The audience was all HI employees. There were 6,844 nonsupervisory employees. First- and second-level managers numbered 655, and the senior management team numbered 41.

Solution

A detailed analysis indicated that the major causes of the problem of sexual harassment were a lack of understanding of the company's sexual harassment policy and a lack of understanding about what constitutes inappropriate and illegal behavior. As a result, a one-day workshop was designed to educate all first- and second-level managers about sexual harassment. After the managers attended the program, they were required to conduct a meeting with employees to disseminate information about the company's policy and to discuss what constitutes inappropriate behavior. In essence, the program reached every employee using this process. Seventeen one-day workshops were conducted over a forty-five-day period, and a total of 655 managers participated.

Figure 3.5. Sexual Harassment Complaints

Figure 3.5. Sexual Harassment Complaints

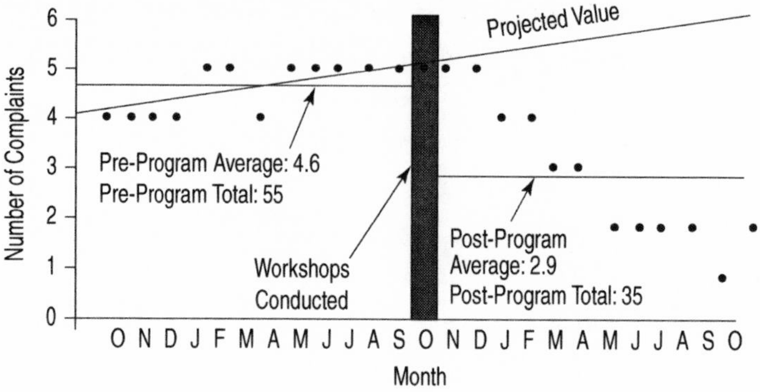

Measures That Matter

Two measures are critical in this analysis. The first measure is the number of internal sexual harassment complaints filed with the human resources manager. These formal written complaints had to be investigated, and some resolution had to be reached, whether sexual harassment was confirmed or not. The second measure is avoidable employee turnover, which represents employees who leave voluntarily and thus is turnover that could have been prevented in some way. Figure 3.5 plots the sexual harassment complaints.

Conditions Test

The human resources staff, including the human resources manager, reviewed HI's climate during the one-year period following the program implementation. The group concluded the following:

- The upward trend of sexual harassment complaints probably would have continued if the company had not implemented the program.

- They could not identify any new influences other than the program that could have prevented the sexual harassment complaints. Therefore, the difference between the projected value based on the trend and the actual end-of-program measurement was the decrease in the number of complaints that could be attributed to the sexual harassment prevention program.

For more details of the HI case study, see *Proving the Value of HR: ROI Case Studies* (Phillips and Phillips, 2007).

Trend Line Analysis Example 3: National Book Company

Setting

National Book Company, a publisher of specialty books, was experiencing productivity problems in its shipping department. On any given day, many of the scheduled shipments were not sent out, which meant that promised shipments to some customers were delayed. The company's organization development staff explored the issue, analyzed the problem, and addressed the issue in a team program.

Audience

The audience was all the employees in the shipping department, including the three supervisors.

Solution

The solution was an off-the-job meeting with an organization development consultant during which the employees of the shipping department explored the problem, its causes, suggestions for improvement, and commitments to make changes. Individual and collective follow-up sessions spanned a two-week period.

Figure 3.6. Shipment Productivity

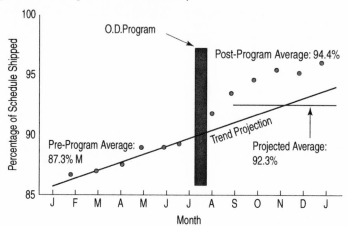

Measures That Matter

The critical measure is shipment productivity—the percentage of scheduled shipments that shipped each day. The results were reported back to the shipping department staff on a routine basis. Figure 3.6 shows the shipment productivity before and after the meeting with the organization development consultant.

Conditions Test

The team members concluded the following:

- The upward trend in shipment productivity prior to the program would probably have continued because of ongoing concern about productivity and discussions of productivity in staff meetings.

- No other new influences on shipment productivity had occurred during the evaluation period, so the total improvement could be attributed to the team-building program. Thus, the difference between the actual average of 94.4 percent and the projected average of

92.3 percent (2.1 percent) represents the improvement directly connected with the program.

Final Thoughts

This chapter shows how simple trend line analysis can be used to isolate the effects of a program. This technique is useful when no new influences other than the program have entered the process during program implementation or subsequently. Trend line analysis is a useful tool, but unfortunately, other processes often do enter the picture; therefore, another isolation technique must used.

Forecasting is a little more complicated than trend line analysis. Its use will be rare because it requires that mathematical relationships between key variables be known or worked out; however, when forecasting can be used, it is a credible method of isolating program effects. If neither trend line analysis nor forecasting can be used, the next step is to consider the use of estimates, which is covered in the next chapter.

References

Armstrong, J. (ed.) *Principles of Forecasting: A Handbook for Researchers and Practitioners*. Boston: Kluwer, 2001.

Phillips, P. P., and Phillips, J. J. *Proving the Value of HR: ROI Case Studies*. Birmingham, Ala.: ROI Institute, 2007.

Salkind, N. *Statistics for People Who (Think They) Hate Statistics*. Thousand Oaks, Calif.: Sage, 2000.

4

Use of Expert Estimates

This chapter moves to a more controversial, yet important set of tools for isolating the effects of programs. Essentially, this approach uses estimates from a variety of experts, among whom the program participants are perhaps the most credible source. The use of estimates has been shunned by some researchers, who contend that if control groups or time series analysis (trend lines or forecasts) cannot be used, no other technique should be attempted. Unfortunately, the need to isolate the effects of a program does not go away just because the preferred tools do not apply. Failure to isolate the effects of a program leaves the owners of that program somewhat vulnerable or at least unable to connect the program to its business impact. Other techniques must be explored in order to at least attempt to get a credible assessment of a program's true impact. In businesses and other organizations with dynamic environments and time constraints, decisions will be made with the best available data. Ultimately, these decisions will be more subjective, not less, to the extent that all reasonable and credible data are not brought to bear.

The good news is that estimates can be phenomenally powerful. A tremendous amount of research shows the effectiveness of expert estimates. When specific guidelines are followed and the estimates are adjusted for error, they become credible and, unfortunately, easy to use. Ease of use is unfortunate when estimates become the method of choice rather than a method of last resort. The methods described in the previous chapters of this book should be considered first, before resorting to estimates. Estimates are not preferred, but evaluators must be prepared to use and defend them when other methods are not available. This chapter explores how estimates can be a powerful and credible way to isolate the effects of a program.

Participants' Estimates of Program Impact

An easily implemented method for isolating the impact of a program is obtaining information directly from the participants. The effectiveness of this approach rests on the assumption that participants are capable of determining or estimating how much of a performance improvement is related to the program. Because their actions have produced the improvement, participants may have accurate input on the issue. They should know how much of the change was caused by applying what they learned in the program. Although it is an estimate, this value will typically have credibility with management because participants are at the center of the change or improvement.

When this technique is used, several assumptions are made:

- The variety of activities, tasks, and learning opportunities that were implemented as a result of the program, project, or initiative were all focused on improving performance.

- One or more business measures were identified prior to program implementation and monitored both before and after the program. Data monitoring has revealed an improvement in the business measure.

- The program needs to be linked to a specific amount of performance improvement, and the monetary impact of

the improvement needs to be calculated. This
information forms the basis for calculating the ROI.

Given these assumptions, the participants can identify the results that are actually linked to the program and provide the data
necessary to develop the ROI. This information can be gathered
through a focus group, an interview, or a questionnaire.

Using Focus Groups to Obtain Participant Estimates

Focus groups work extremely well for isolating the effects of a program if the groups can be kept relatively small—eight to twelve
participants. If they become much larger, the groups should be divided into smaller groups. Focus groups provide an opportunity for
members to share information equally, avoiding domination by any
one individual. The process taps the input, creativity, and reactions
of all the group members.

The participants in a focus group should be the most credible
source of data, according to Guiding Principle 3 of the ROI Methodology. Although some may question the ability of participants to
provide these data, if the situation is examined realistically, one can
see that it is their performance that is being scrutinized. They often
know which influences have caused their performance to improve
and, to a certain degree, the relationship between those influences
and the outcomes. Even if they are not the ideal source of data, they
are often the most credible in comparison with other sources. This is
particularly true when the participants are professional, technical,
clerical, or managerial employees.

The meeting should take about one hour (slightly more if multiple factors affected the results or if multiple business measures are
being evaluated). The facilitator should be neutral during the process. (For example, an individual with an ownership role in the
program should not conduct the focus group.) Focus group facilitation and input should be as objective as possible.

The task is to link the business results with the program. The group is presented with the improvement (a fact) and asked to provide input in order to determine the impact of the program on the given improvement.

To arrive at the most credible value for the program's impact, follow these steps:

1. *Explain the purpose of the focus group meeting.* Participants should understand that their team has achieved a specific improvement in performance. While many factors could have contributed to the performance, the task of the focus group is to determine how much of the improvement is related to the program.

2. *Discuss the rules.* Each participant should be encouraged to provide input, limiting his or her comments to two minutes (or less) for each specific factor. Comments are confidential and will not be linked to an individual.

3. *Explain the importance of the process.* The participants' role in the process is critical. Because it is their performance that has improved, participants are in the best position to indicate what caused the improvement; they are the experts in this determination. Without quality input, the contribution of the program (or other processes) may never be known.

4. *Identify the measure, and show the improvement.* Using actual data, present the level of performance before and after the program, showing the change in business results.

5. *Identify the different factors that may have contributed to the performance improvement.* Using input from experts—others who are knowledgeable about the setting and improvements—list any factors that may have influenced the improvement (for example, a change in the volume of work, a new work system or procedure, or enhanced technology).

6. *Ask the group to identify other factors that may have contributed to the performance improvement.* In some situations, only the

participants know of other influencing factors, and those factors should surface at this time. If any other factors are identified, they should be added to the list. At this point, all the factors should have been identified.

7. *Discuss the links.* Taking one factor at a time, have participants individually describe the link between that factor and the business results. For example, for the training influence, participants would describe how the training program has driven improvement by providing examples, anecdotes, and other supporting evidence. All participants should be allowed the same amount of time. Participants may require some prompting to provide comments. If they cannot provide dialogue regarding an issue, there is a good chance that the factor had little or no influence.

8. *Repeat step 7 for each factor.* Explore each factor until all the participants have discussed the linkage between all the factors and the business performance improvement. After the linkages have been discussed, the participants should have a clear understanding of the cause-and-effect relationships between the various factors and the business impact.

9. *Ask participants to allocate a percentage of the improvement to each of the factors discussed.* Provide participants with a pie chart that represents the total amount of improvement for the measure in question, then ask them to carve up the pie, allocating a percentage to each improvement, making sure that the percentages total 100 percent. Some participants may feel uncertain about this process, but they should be encouraged to complete it, using their best estimates. Let them know that their uncertainty will be addressed in the next step.

10. *Ask for confidence estimates.* Ask participants to review their allocations and, for each one, to estimate their level of confidence in each allocation estimate. Using a scale of 0 to 100 percent, in which 0 percent represents no confidence and 100 percent is certainty, have participants express their level

of confidence for each of their estimates in step 9. A participant may be more comfortable with some factors than others, so the confidence estimates may vary. Results will be adjusted according to these confidence estimates.

11. *Ask participants to multiply the two percentages.* For example, if an individual has allocated 30 percent of the improvement to a specific program and is 80 percent confident, she would multiply 30 percent by 80 percent, which results in 24 percent. In essence, the participant is suggesting that at least 24 percent of the team's business improvement is linked to the program. The confidence estimate provides a conservative discount factor, allowing evaluators to adjust for error in the estimate. The pie charts, with the calculations, are collected without names to identify the participants, and the calculations are verified. Another option is to collect the pie charts and make the calculations for the participants.

12. *Report the results.* The average of the adjusted values for the group should be developed and communicated to the group, if possible. Also, a summary of all the information should be communicated to the participants as soon as possible.

Participants who do not provide information should be excluded from the analysis. Table 4.1 illustrates the approach discussed here with an example of one participant's estimates.

The participant allocated 50 percent of the improvement to the training program. The confidence percentage represents the participant's perception of how much error there could be in the estimate. A 70 percent confidence level equates to a potential error range of $\pm$ 30 percent (100% – 70% = 30%). The amount of improvement caused by the training program could be 30 percent more (50% + 15% = 65%), 30 percent less (50% – 15% = 35%), or somewhere in between. Therefore, the participant's allocation is in the range of 35 percent to 65 percent. In essence, the confidence

Table 4.1. One Participant's Estimates

Factor That Influenced Improvement	Percentage of Improvement Caused by Factor	Level of Confidence, Expressed as a Percentage
Training program	50%	70%
Adjustment in procedures	10%	80%
Change in technology	10%	50%
Revision of incentive plan	20%	90%
Increased management attention	10%	50%
Other _____	___%	___%
Total	100%	

estimate frames an error range. To be conservative, the low value of the range (35 percent) is used, following Guiding Principle 7: Adjust estimates of improvement for potential errors of estimation.

The approach described in the preceding paragraph is equivalent to multiplying the isolation estimate by the confidence percentage to develop a usable program factor value of 35 percent (50% × 70%). This adjusted percentage is then multiplied by the actual amount of improvement (post-program value minus pre-program value) to isolate the portion attributed to the program. The adjusted value of improvement attributed to the program is now ready for conversion to monetary values and, ultimately, for use in calculating the return on investment.

The approach detailed in this section provides a credible way to isolate the effects of a program when other methods will not work. It is often regarded as a low-cost solution to the problem of isolation because it takes only a few focus groups and a small amount of time to arrive at a conclusion. In most settings, the conversion to monetary values is not performed by the group but developed in another way. For most data, the company may already have developed a standard conversion rate. The issues involved in converting data to monetary values are detailed in *Data Conversion*, the next book in this series. However, if necessary, participants can provide input on the monetary value of the improvement during the same focus group meeting in which they provide their factor allocations. The steps for estimating monetary values are similar to the steps for estimating program effects.

Using Questionnaires to Obtain Participant Estimates

Sometimes, focus groups are not an available option or are considered unacceptable for collecting data. The participants may not be available for a group meeting, or focus groups may be too expensive. In these situations, a follow-up questionnaire may be administered to collect similar information. By answering a series of questions about the program's impact, participants address the same issues that they would deal with in a focus group.

The questionnaire may focus solely on the issue of isolating the effects of the program, or it may focus on the monetary value derived from the program, so that the information pertaining to the isolation issue is only a part of the data collected. The latter is a more versatile way to use questionnaires when it is not certain exactly how participants will provide business impact data. In some programs, the precise measures that will be influenced by the program may not be known. This is sometimes the case in programs involving leadership, process improvement teams, communications, negotiation, problem solving, innovation, or performance improvement initiatives. In these situations, it is helpful to obtain information from participants through a series of questions about how they have used what they have learned and the subsequent impact on their work or team. It is important for participants to know about these questions before they receive the questionnaire; the surprise element can be disastrous in data collection. Allowing participants to preview the questions early in the program will help them provide better data later on. A recommended series of questions is shown in Exhibit 4.1.

Exhibit 4.1. Questions for Participants Who Are Estimating Program Impact

1. How have you and your job changed as a result of your participation in this program (skills and knowledge application)?

2. What impact do these changes bring to your work or work unit?

3. How is this impact measured (specific measure)?

4. How much did the value of this measure change after you participated in the program (monthly, weekly, or daily amount)?

5. What is the unit value of the measure?

6. What is the basis for this unit value? Please indicate the assumptions made and the specific calculations you performed to arrive at the value.

7. What is the annual value of this change or improvement in your work unit (for the first year)?

8. Recognizing that many factors besides this program may have influenced the output results, please identify other factors that could have contributed to this performance improvement.

9. What percentage of this improvement can be attributed directly to the application of skills and knowledge gained during the program? (0–100%)

10. What confidence do you have in the estimate and data provided for Question 9, expressed as a percentage? (0% = no confidence; 100% = certainty)

11. What other individuals or groups could estimate this percentage or determine the amount?

Perhaps an illustration of the process of using a questionnaire to gather participant estimates of business impact will reveal its effectiveness and acceptability. In a global auto rental company, the impact of a leadership program for new managers was being assessed. Because the decision to calculate the impact of the program was made after it had begun, the control group arrangement was not a feasible method for isolating the effects of the program. A specific business impact measure that was directly linked to the program had not been identified, so participants could select two measures to improve. As a result, using trend line analysis was not appropriate because there were too many measures. Participants' estimates proved to be the most useful way to assess the impact of the program on business performance.

In a detailed follow-up questionnaire, participants were asked a variety of questions about the application and impact of what was learned in the program. The series of questions listed in Exhibit 4.1 provided an assessment of the impact.

Although this series of questions is challenging, when set up properly and presented to participants in an appropriate way, such questions can be very effective for collecting impact data. Table 4.2 shows a sample of the calculations based on these questions for this particular program. In this example, twenty-nine participants were asked to identify two measures for improvement. The table shows the input from fifteen of the twenty-nine. The first column represents the participant who responded (the list is in random order). The second column represents data for Question 7 in Exhibit 4.1; the next five columns represent input for Questions 3, 6, 9, 8, and 10. The last column provides the adjusted monetary value for each measure identified by each participant. These first fifteen measures are added to get the total monetary benefit for these measures. The total contribution of the remaining fourteen of the participants' first measures and the total for the second measure are also shown. Each measure is converted to money, linked to the program through estimation with an adjustment made for error,

Table 4.2. Sample of Input from Participants in a Leadership Program for New Managers

Participant Number	Q7 Annual Improvement	Q3 Measure	Q6 Method for Converting Data to Monetary Value	Q9 Contribution from Program	Q8 Number of Other Factors	Q10 Confidence Estimate	Q7×Q9×Q10 Total Monetary Benefit (Adjusted Value)
1	$13,100	Sales	Standard	60%	3	80%	$6,288
3	41,200	Productivity	Expert	75%	1	95%	29,355
4	5,300	Sales	Standard	80%	1	90%	3,816
6	7,210	Cost	N/A	70%	2	70%	3,533
9	4,215	Efficiency	Standard	40%	3	75%	1,265
10	17,500	Quality	Expert	35%	4	60%	3,675
12	11,500	Time	Standard	60%	2	80%	5,520
14	3,948	Time	Standard	70%	1	80%	2,211
15	14,725	Sales	Standard	40%	3	70%	4,123
17	6,673	Efficiency	Estimate	50%	3	60%	2,002
18	12,140	Cost	N/A	100%	0	100%	12,140
19	17,850	Sales	Standard	60%	2	70%	7,497
21	13,920	Sales	Standard	50%	3	80%	5,568
22	15,362	Cost	N/A	40%	4	90%	5,530
23	18,923	Sales	Standard	60%	1	75%	8,515

Total for the items above		$101,038
Total for the next 14 items		$84,398
Total for 2nd measure		$143,764
Total benefits		$329,200

and adjusted appropriately, then the amounts are added together to provide the total contribution to the organization. The total value for the program represents the total of the input from all who provided data, following Guiding Principle 6: If no improvement data are available for a population or from a specific source, assume that little or no improvement has occurred. That is, only the data provided were used.

Although these input data are estimates, the approach has an acceptable level of accuracy and credibility. Remember, this technique is a worst-case scenario. Four adjustments have been used to constitute a conservative and thus more credible approach.

1. The individuals who do not respond to the questionnaire or do not provide usable data on the questionnaire are assumed to have no improvements to report. This is probably an overstatement because some individuals will experience improvements but not report them on the questionnaire or not respond to the questionnaire. This adjustment follows Guiding Principle 6, which is discussed in *ROI Fundamentals*, the first book in this series.

2. Extreme data and incomplete or unsupported claims are omitted from the analysis, although they may be included in an "other benefits" category. (Guiding Principle 8)

3. Because only annualized values are used, it is assumed that no benefits from the program occur after the first year of implementation. In reality, leadership development would be expected to add value for several years after the program has been conducted. (Guiding Principle 9)

4. The confidence estimates, expressed as percentages, are multiplied by the improvement values to reduce the amount of the improvement according to the potential error in the estimates. (Guiding Principle 7)

When presented to senior management, the results of this impact study were perceived to be an understatement of the program's success; the data and the process were considered credible.

Collecting an adequate amount of quality data from the series of impact questions is the critical challenge in using questionnaires to collect participant estimates of program impact. Participants must be primed to provide usable data. *Data Collection*, the second book in this series, provides a detailed list of techniques for obtaining a high response rate. Seven techniques are powerful in securing a large return rate (60 to 90 percent).

1. Participants should know in advance that they are expected to provide detailed data and should be given an explanation of why the data are needed and how they will be used.

2. Participants should see a copy of the questionnaire and discuss it while they are involved in the program. If possible, a verbal commitment to provide the data should be obtained at that time.

3. Participants should be reminded of the requirement to provide data prior to the data collection period. The reminder should come from others involved in the process—for example, from the participants' immediate manager.

4. Participants can be provided with examples of how the questionnaire can be completed, using most-likely scenarios and typical data.

5. One or more incentives can be used to stimulate a return.

6. The participants' immediate manager should support, encourage, or be involved in data collection.

7. Participants should be provided with a summary of the data once it is compiled.

Use of these techniques keeps the data collection process, with its chain of impact questions, from being a surprise and accomplishes three critical tasks:

1. *Increases the response rate.* Because participants have committed to providing data during the session, a greater percentage will respond.

2. *Increases the quantity of data.* Because participants will understand the chain of impact and how the data will be used, they will complete more questions.

3. *Improves the quality of the data.* Because expectations are clarified up front, participants have a greater understanding of the type of data needed and improved confidence in the data they provide. Perhaps subconsciously, participants begin to think through the consequences of the program on specific impact measures. The result: improved quality of input.

Using Interviews to Obtain Participant Estimates

In lieu of a questionnaire, an interview can be useful for isolating the effects of a program. An interview may represent a compromise between using a focus group and using a questionnaire. A focus group may not be feasible; perhaps it is not feasible for a significant number of participants to reconvene. Using a questionnaire is easier than using a focus group; participant data for the purpose of isolating program effects can be gathered simply by adding three questions. However, an interview may be far more revealing and useful than a questionnaire and can be conducted by telephone, which is easier than convening a focus group. Of course, a face-to-face interview is more powerful, but it may be too expensive. Essentially, the line of questioning in an interview is similar to that on a questionnaire. To isolate the effects of a program, the same three questions as would be added to a questionnaire can be added to an interview.

Advantages and Disadvantages of Participant Estimates

Participant estimation is an important technique for isolating the effect of a program. However, the process has some disadvantages. It is an estimate and, consequently, does not have the accuracy desired by some professionals. Also, the input data may be unreliable because some participants are incapable of providing these types of estimates. They might not be aware of exactly which factors contributed to the results, or they may be reluctant to provide data. If the questions come as a surprise, the data will be scarce.

Several advantages make participant estimation attractive. It is a simple process, easily understood by most participants and by those who review evaluation data. It is inexpensive and takes very little time and analysis, making the results an efficient addition to the evaluation process. Participant estimates originate from a credible source—the individuals who actually produced the improvement.

The advantages usually offset the disadvantages. Isolating the effects of a program will never be a precise process, and participant estimates are accurate enough for clients and management groups. Participant estimates are appropriate when the participants are managers, supervisors, team leaders, sales associates, engineers, or other professional and technical employees.

Participant estimates are the default isolation method for many types of programs. If nothing else will work, this method is used. A fallback approach is needed if the effect of the program must always be isolated, which is recommended. The reluctance to use this process often rests with the evaluator and his or her immediate manager or with staff and support team members, who typically avoid estimates because they are reluctant to use a technique that is not airtight. However, the key audience for the data—sponsors, clients, or senior executives—will readily accept this approach. Living in an ambiguous world, they understand that estimates have to be made and may be the only way to approach the issue of isolation. They understand the challenge and appreciate the conservative approach, often commenting that the actual value of a program is probably greater than the value presented. Because of the factors outlined here, approximately 50 percent of the published studies on the ROI Methodology use participant estimates to isolate the effects of programs.

Case Study

To show how the estimation process works within an organization, it is best to examine an actual case. This case study shows the power of developing estimates from a group of participants involved in different processes, all with different process owners.

Setting

National Bank had established a carefully planned growth pattern through acquisitions of smaller banks. One recent acquisition was quite large, representing almost $1 billion in total assets. After the acquisition, record-keeping systems and performance-monitoring processes were implemented at all locations. Each branch in the network had a scorecard on which performance was tracked, using several measures such as new accounts, total deposits, and sales growth of specific products. National Bank had an excellent reputation as an organization with a strong sales culture. Through a sales training program, all branch personnel were taught how to aggressively pursue new customers and cross-sell to existing customers in a variety of product lines. The bank used sales training coupled with incentives and management reinforcement to ensure that ambitious sales goals were met. A variety of marketing initiatives also supported the sales process. Six months after the systems were in place in the new acquisition, management was ready to implement the sales culture among all branch personnel.

Audience

The audience was the employees in all thirty new branches. At each branch, the branch manager and the teller supervisors were included in the program, bringing the total to over six hundred participants.

Solution

Recognizing that several factors had influenced the scorecard results, management decided to let the program participants estimate the impact of the program in a focus group facilitated by the branch managers. Branch management initially identified that sales output had been significantly influenced by the following factors: (1) the sales training program, (2) incentive systems, (3) management emphasis on sales and management reinforcement of sales activities, and (4) marketing. After the program was implemented, management tracked performance improvements on the scorecard by product category.

The sales training program covered both product knowledge (products had been adjusted slightly from product offerings prior to the acquisition) and sales techniques (explaining the features and benefits of the products, overcoming resistance to the sale, and pointing out advantages over competitors' products). The program was delivered in half-day increments for a total of one and a half days.

The incentive system for the branch staff who sold credit cards changed slightly under the new ownership. The incentive process was owned by the compensation department. The bonus for selling a credit card was not large, but for some, it was a motivator to sell more. For others, it may not have made much difference.

The goal-setting and reinforcement process was owned by the organization development department. Previously, the employees had had goals, but the goals had not been as detailed as those required after the acquisition. Under the new ownership, goals (which were posted in each branch's break room) were specified by individual and by product line for each day. Each morning, the branch manager had a brief meeting with the staff to discuss the goals that must be achieved that day. At the end of each day, there was a brief review of progress made and a discussion of what could be done to make up for any deficiencies.

The fourth influence on sales output was marketing. Post-acquisition marketing had been low-key. Signs had been changed, and customers had been welcomed to the new company. There had been no specific promotions or advertising beyond those elements. Still, the marketing had had an effect; it had brought existing customers into the branch. Perhaps the newly posted signs had even attracted some new customers. These marketing elements were owned by the marketing department, of course.

Measures

Each branch monitored all major measures, including the number of new credit cards, the number of new checking accounts, increases in deposits, and increases in consumer loans. Although other measures were related to the products, these were the measures that the staff could most directly influence.

Estimates Provided

All participants provided estimates (by branch) in focus groups. Each branch manager was trained in the focus group process and conducted the meeting for his or her branch. The data from each of the thirty branches were captured in this way. Branch managers were considered independent of the change processes, a requirement for being the focus group facilitator. Each manager collected input from his or her entire group, using a summary of estimates for each measure.

Credibility Check

To ensure that the most credible individuals provided estimates, the evaluation team decided that branch staff members should provide the data. It was their performance that was being evaluated, and they should know more than anyone else what had caused their performance to improve.

Methodology

The branch managers in the target metro area conducted focus groups with the team to estimate the percentage of improvement that could be attributed to each of the four influences listed earlier. All branch employees provided input during a meeting facilitated by their branch manager. In each carefully organized meeting, the branch manager

- Described the task.

- Explained why the information was needed and how it would be used.

- Had employees discuss the link between each factor and the specific output measure.

- Provided employees with any additional information needed to estimate the contribution of each factor.

- Asked employees to identify any other influences that may have contributed to the increase.

- Obtained from each employee an estimate of the contribution of each factor. The total had to be 100 percent. Several consensus-reaching tools were offered.

- Obtained the confidence level of each employee for his or her estimate on each factor (100 percent = certainty; 0 percent = no confidence). The values of the estimates and confidence levels were averaged for each factor.

For example, Table 4.3 shows the information collected from one branch for one business measure, the increase in credit-card accounts.

The amount of improvement attributed to the first factor, the sales training program, was determined by multiplying the to-tal amount of improvement (175) by the average percentage of

**Table 4.3. One Branch's Allocation of Factors Affecting
Number of Credit Accounts, and Corresponding
Confidence Levels**

Contributing Factor	Average Impact on Results	Average Confidence Level
Sales training program	32%	83%
Incentive systems	41%	87%
Goal setting, management emphasis on sales	14%	62%
Marketing	11%	75%
Other	2%	91%
	100%	

Note: Monthly increase in credit card accounts: 175.

performance attributed to the sales training program (32%). This calculation shows the impact of the program on the credit-card product line. The number was then adjusted by the confidence percentage (83%). Thus, the number of new credit cards attributed to the sales training program was $175 \times 32\% \times 83\% = 46$ (at least). If the same calculation is made for every factor, the total is less than the original 175. In essence, "the error" is removed from the analysis.

Immediate Managers' Estimates of Program Impact

In lieu of (or in addition to) participant estimates, the participants' immediate managers may be asked to assess the extent of a program's role in producing a performance improvement. In some settings, participants' managers may be more familiar with the other factors influencing performance and thus may be better equipped to provide estimates of impact.

After describing the improvement made by a program's participants, ask their supervisors these questions:

1. In addition to this program, what factors could have contributed to this success?

2. What percentage of the performance improvement was a result of the program? (0% to 100%)

3. What is the basis for this estimate?

4. What is your confidence in this estimate, expressed as a percentage? (0 percent = no confidence; 100 percent = complete confidence)

5. What other individuals or groups would know about this improvement and could estimate the percentage of improvement that resulted from the program?

These questions are similar to those asked of participants. Immediate managers' estimates should be analyzed in the same way as participant estimates. To provide a more conservative evaluation, estimates should be adjusted by the confidence percentage. If feasible, it is recommended that input be obtained from both participants and supervisors. If both participants' and supervisors' estimates have been collected, evaluators must decide which estimates to use. If one type of estimate is more credible than another, the more credible one should be used. The most conservative approach is to use the estimate that yields the lowest value and include an appropriate explanation (Guiding Principle 4). Another option is to recognize that each source has its own unique perspective and that an average of the two is appropriate, placing equal weight on each input.

Supervisor estimates have the same disadvantages as participant estimates. They are subjective and therefore may be viewed with skepticism by some. Supervisors may be reluctant to participate or may be incapable of providing accurate impact estimates. They may not know about factors other than the program that may have contributed to the improvement, unless they work closely with the participants they manage.

The advantages of supervisor estimates are similar to the advantages of participant estimation. They are simple and inexpensive and have an acceptable degree of credibility because they come from the managers of those who participated in the program and made the improvements. When supervisor estimates are combined with participant estimates, their credibility may be enhanced. Also, when levels of confidence are used to adjust the results, the credibility of supervisor estimates further increases.

Senior Management's Estimates of Program Impact

In some cases, upper management may estimate the percentage of improvement that should be attributed to the program. For example, in one organization, the senior management team adjusted the results from a program to create self-directed teams. After considering factors external to the program that could have contributed to performance improvement, such as technology, procedures, and process change, management applied a subjective factor of 60 percent to represent the portion of the results that should be attributed to the program. The factor of 60 percent was developed in a meeting with top managers and thus had the benefit of group ownership. Although estimates by top management can be highly subjective, often they represent input from the individuals who approve or provide the funding for a program. Sometimes, their level of comfort with the process is the most important consideration.

Because of their highly subjective nature, senior management estimates of program contributions are not usually recommended. Senior managers may not understand all the factors that could have affected the business measure driven by a program or may have no indication of the relative impact of the factors. Therefore, top management estimates should be avoided or used only when necessary to secure buy-in from the senior management team.

In some situations, a large program impact results in a very high ROI. Top managers may feel more comfortable with the evaluation if they are allowed to adjust the results, even if actual data rather than estimates were used as the basis for the ROI evaluation. Their basis for the adjustment is their perception that the numbers are unrealistic. In essence, they are applying a discount to adjust for an unknown factor, even though attempts have been made to identify each factor. While there is no scientific basis for this technique, discounting the data sometimes helps secure management buy-in.

Customers' Estimates of Program Impact

One helpful approach in some highly specific situations is soliciting input on a program's impact directly from customers. Customers can be asked why they chose a particular product or service or to explain how individuals applying skills and abilities have influenced their reaction to a product or service. This technique focuses directly on what the program is designed to improve. For example, after a teller training program was conducted consequent to a bank merger, market survey data showed that the percentage of customers who were dissatisfied with teller knowledge was reduced by 5 percent compared with market survey data before the training program. Since only the training program had increased teller knowledge, the 5 percent reduction in dissatisfied customers was directly attributable to the program.

In another example, a large real estate company provided a comprehensive training program for agents, focusing on presentation skills. As customers listed their homes with an agent, they received a survey that explored their reasons for deciding to list their home with the company. Among the reasons listed were the presentation skills of the agent. Responses to this question and related questions provided evidence of new listings that could be attributed to the training program.

Of course, customer estimates can be used only in situations in which customer input can be obtained. Even then, customers may not be able to provide accurate data. They must be able to see the influencing factors in order to isolate them. However, because customer input is usually credible, the approach is effective when the situation allows it to be used.

Experts' Estimates of Program Impact

External or internal experts can sometimes estimate the portion of results that can be attributed to a program. When this strategy is used, experts must be selected on the basis of their knowledge of the process, program, and situation. For example, an expert might be able to provide estimates of how much change in a quality measure can be attributed to a specific program such as Six Sigma or continuous quality improvement.

Expert estimates would most likely be used to evaluate the success of a program implemented by an external supplier. In previous evaluations, a certain portion of the results would have been attributed to the program. This percentage, provided by the supplier, is extrapolated to the current situation. This approach should be pursued cautiously because the current situation may be very different from those in the supplier's past implementations. However, if the previous program applications have many similarities to the current situation, the supplier's value may be used as a rough estimate. Because of the concerns listed here, this approach should be used with explanations. In addition, it is important to check the supplier's studies, to ensure that credible, objective processes were used for data collection and analysis.

The use of expert estimates has one advantage: its credibility often reflects the reputation of the expert or independent consultant. It can provide quick input from a reputable source. Sometimes, top management will place more confidence in external experts than in their own internal staff.

Determining the Impact of Other Factors

In some situations, it may be feasible to calculate the impact of factors other than the program in question and then credit the implemented program with the remaining portion. In this approach, the program takes credit for improvement that cannot be attributed to other factors.

An example will help explain the approach. In a large bank, a significant increase in consumer loan volume was generated after a training program was conducted for consumer loan officers. Part of the increase was attributed to the program, and the remainder was attributed to the influence of other factors operating during the same time period. Two other factors were identified by the evaluator: a loan officer's production improves with time, and falling interest rates stimulated an increase in consumer loans.

The first factor considers the fact that the confidence of loan officers improves as they make loans. They use consumer lending policy manuals and gain knowledge and expertise through trial and error. The contribution of this factor to performance improvement was estimated by using input from several internal experts in the marketing department.

For the second factor, industry sources were used to show the relationship between increased consumer loan volume and falling interest rates.

The estimates based on the first and second factors accounted for a certain percentage of increased consumer loan volume. The remaining improvement was attributed to the training program.

The method of isolation by elimination is appropriate when the factors external to the program are easily identified and appropriate mechanisms are available to calculate their impact on the improvement. In some cases, estimating the impact of other factors is just as difficult as estimating the impact of the program in question, leaving this approach less advantageous. This process can be credible if the method used to isolate the impact of the other factors is credible.

Estimate Example 1: Global Financial Services

Setting

Global Financial Services, Inc. (GFS) is a large international firm that offers a variety of financial services to clients. Analyzing its current sales practices and results, the firm identified a need to manage sales relationships more effectively. A task force comprising representatives from field sales, marketing, financial consulting, information technology, and education and training examined several solutions for improving relationships, including customer contact software packages. The firm chose to implement a software package called ACT!™. This software, developed by Symantec and designed to turn contacts into relationships and relationships into increased sales, features a flexible customer database, easy contact entry, a calendar, and a to-do list. ACT! enabled quick and effective customer communication and was designed for use with customized reports. It also had built-in contact and calendar sharing and was Internet-ready.

Audience and Solution

The audience consisted of 4,000 relationship managers. These managers were sales representatives who had direct contact with customers. GFS evaluated the success of the software on a pilot basis, using three groups, each composed of thirty relationship managers. A one-day workshop was designed to teach the relationship managers how to use the software. The ACT! software was distributed and used at the workshop. If the trial program proved successful, yielding an appropriate return on investment, GFS planned to implement ACT! for all its relationship managers.

Measures

Measures were tracked in four categories:

1. Increase in sales to existing customers
2. Reduction of customer complaints about missed deadlines, late responses, and failure to complete transactions
3. Increase in customer satisfaction on the customer survey
4. Reduction in response time on customer inquiries and requests

Estimates Provided

The relationship managers provided estimates of program impact in a focus group meeting. Five groups of twelve—a total of sixty managers—participated. It was decided that the relationship managers were the most credible source of data for this estimate. Their performance was being judged; therefore, they should know the program's impact better than anyone. The method for the estimate was the focus group approach outlined earlier in this chapter.

Estimate Example 2: Cracker Box

Setting

Cracker Box, Inc., was a large, fast-growing restaurant chain located along interstate highways and major thoroughfares. In the past ten years, Cracker Box had grown steadily; it had over four hundred stores and plans for continued growth. Each store had a restaurant and a gift shop. A store manager was responsible for both profit units. Store manager turnover was approximately 25 percent—lower than the industry average of 35 percent but still excessive. Because of the chain's growth and the rate of manager turnover, almost two hundred new store managers had to be developed each year.

Store managers operated autonomously and were held accountable for store performance. Using their store team, managers controlled expenses, monitored operating results, and took action as needed to improve store performance. Each store tracked dozens of performance measures in a monthly operating report. Some measures were reported weekly.

Store managers were recruited both internally and externally and had to have restaurant experience. Many had college degrees. The program for new managers usually lasted nine months. When selected, the store manager trainee reported directly to a store manager who served as a mentor to the trainee. Trainees were usually assigned to a specific store location for the duration of manager training. During the training period, the entire store team reported to the manager trainee as the store manager coached the trainee. As part of the formal training and development, each manager trainee was required to attend at least three one-week programs offered by the company's corporate university. One such program was the Performance Management Program.

Audience and Solution

The audience consisted of new store managers (store manager trainees) who were attending the Performance Management Program as part of the nine-month training program.

The Performance Management Program taught new store managers how to improve store performance. Participants learned how to establish measurable goals for employees, provide performance feedback, measure progress toward goals, and take action to ensure that goals were met. The program focused on using the store team to solve problems and improve performance. Problem analysis and counseling skills were also covered. The one-week program was residential, and evening assignments were often part of the process. Skill practice sessions were integrated with the other sessions during the week. The program was taught by both the corporate university staff and operation managers. Program sessions took place at the corporate university near the company's headquarters.

Measures

The measures in this example varied, depending on where the manager was located and what operational issues were a concern to both the manager and his or her direct supervisor. Measures could include sales and customer service, store operations, efficiency, safety and health, absenteeism and turnover, or any others that were appropriate.

Estimates Provided

The manager trainees provided the estimates. Essentially, it was each store team's performance that was being measured, and the teams reported directly to the manager trainees. The evaluation team concluded that the manager trainees were the most credible source of information about the factors that could have contributed to their store's improvement. The data were obtained on an action planning document, on which each manager trainee was asked to indicate the percentage of improvement directly related to the program. Confidence levels were also provided and were used to adjust the amount of improvement reported.

For more details on this case, see *Proving the Value of HR: ROI Case Studies* (Phillips and Phillips, 2007).

Estimate Example 3: Public Bank of Malaysia

Setting

The Public Bank of Malaysia began offering a new deposit savings product and was interested in measuring the impact of the new product on business performance.

Audience and Solution

A training program on the new product targeted customer service representatives. The training focused on ways to sell the new deposit savings product by convincing customers to buy it.

Measure

The only measure was sales of the deposit savings product.

Estimates Provided

When customers decided to put their money into the new savings product, they were asked to complete a card and leave it in a box as they exited the branch. The card listed reasons why a customer might have selected the product at that time. The customer could check any or all of these factors. One of the factors was the sales approach of the customer service representative, which might have convinced a customer to buy the product. The responses on this factor would be directly related to the training program, assuming that no other factors had influenced the customer service representatives' sales skills. The use of customer estimates often carries a great deal of credibility. However, customers may not be as objective or as accurate as employees in understanding customer choices. The impact of estimates and how they can add credibility has been underscored in other sections of this chapter.

Estimate Example 4: Multi-National, Inc.

Setting

Multi-National, Inc. (MNI) is a large global firm with manufacturing and support facilities in more than twenty-five countries. MNI had experienced tremendous growth and was poised for additional growth in the future. MNI's comprehensive executive development process included a series of programs for the executives. One executive education program, Leadership and Shareholder Value, focused on using leadership and management principles to add shareholder value to the company.

As the program was developed, the company's chief financial officer (CFO) was asked to sponsor it. Because he found the program intriguing, the CFO accepted the challenge and became involved in some of the design issues and the implementation of the program. He made personal visits to as many programs as he could fit into his schedule. His work with the program turned into enthusiasm as he saw an opportunity for an education program to have a measurable business impact, something that he had not seen previously.

Audience, Solution, and Measures

Executives from various functions were the targeted group. Built into the three-day program was a detailed action plan that participants had to develop and implement. The action plan focused on a project to be completed that would add shareholder value to the company. The specific measures influenced included output, quality, cycle time, and customer service.

Because of his enthusiasm about the program and his sincere belief that it was adding significant value to the company, the CFO asked the program designers to follow up on the action plans and determine the success of the program in monetary terms. Two groups were targeted and contacted in order to obtain information on their accomplishments related to the action planning process. Much to the CFO's pleasure, significant improvements were identified as important projects were implemented as a result of the program. Input from the participants was reviewed, and the project items were tallied. To be consistent, only annual values converted to margin were used in the analysis. It was assumed that all the improvements reported were linked directly to the program. The total came to a surprising $3 million for the two groups.

The CFO was unsure of the actual cost of the program but was quite convinced that its benefits exceeded the costs. Eager to show the success of the program, he sent a brief report to senior executives, highlighting the success of the program. Because the executive group had never seen monetary values attached to this type of program, their response was extremely favorable.

Estimates Provided

The CFO was uncomfortable with claiming all the results. He consulted with the leadership development team to explore ways to make the results more credible. The team decided to make two adjustments to the data. In a follow-up e-mail, the participating executives were asked to indicate the percentage of the results that were attributable to the program and their confidence in that allocation, using a scale of 0 to 100 percent. The value of each participant's improvement was adjusted by the percentage attributable to the program and by the confidence percentage. After these adjustments, the total value of the improvements reported by the participants was $950,000. The team assembled the total, fully loaded costs of the program to compare against the benefits and then calculated the ROI, which turned out to be an impressive 87 percent. The CFO felt much better about the results and sent a revised summary to the executive group.

The Power of Estimates

The use of estimates can be a powerful process when the estimates are collected properly, analyzed conservatively, and reported cautiously.

Research

A tremendous amount of research has been compiled on the power of estimates through our work at the ROI Institute and through direct involvement in hundreds of studies. The research suggests that estimates are used in addition to more credible techniques such as control groups and trend line analysis. In the vast majority of cases, using estimates is a conservative and credible approach to isolating the effects of a program. Whenever a control group or trend line analysis is used, estimates should also be used. This provides an opportunity to compare the effectiveness of the estimates with that of more credible methods.

A Demonstration

The power of estimates can be validated in many ways; one of the most effective is to have participants take part in an exercise, especially if a group of individuals has questioned the validity of estimates. The exercise should be discussed for a few minutes and then administered. It takes about ten minutes.

First, pick a measurable fact with a value that the participants will not know precisely but will be able to make a reasonable guess at. A typical example is the distance from the meeting room to the nearest airport, assuming that each individual has been to the airport and thus is capable of providing an estimate. The specific route to the airport should be discussed, examining multiple alternatives, so that all the individuals attempt to estimate the mileage for the same route. Have each participant estimate the mileage and then provide a confidence estimate. Collect all the estimates. Using an Excel spreadsheet, calculate the average of the mileage. Now adjust the estimates based on the confidence levels (multiply the estimated mileage by the confidence percentage), and calculate the adjusted average.

Next, use a mapping service (such as Google Maps or MapQuest) to calculate the precise distance from the meeting room to the airport. Then report the results to the participants. In over two hundred iterations of this exercise, the results have been the same. The estimates before adjustments are made overstate the actual mileage, and the estimates after adjustments are made understate the mileage. This exercise demonstrates what must be done with real estimates; confidence levels must be used to adjust the estimate and provide a conservative result. This quick exercise has even been used during presentations of evaluation results to management groups to show them how powerful and credible estimates can be.

Participant Reaction

Based on the use of estimates in thousands of situations, some interesting conclusions have been drawn about the reaction of participants. Some professionals fear that participants may be unwilling or unable to provide the estimates and may become frustrated or irritated or just not participate. That has not been the case. Participants appreciate being recognized as the authority, the most credible source. They will usually participate, often eagerly, and anxiously await the results of the evaluation. This finding dispels concerns about reluctance on the part of participants.

Management Reaction

One of the fears about using estimates is that management may reject the process and, therefore, the results. This, too, has not been the case. Senior managers understand the difficulty of isolating the effects of a program, especially when many factors are involved. They also realize that the other, more credible techniques may not be appropriate in all cases. They appreciate the way in which the data have been collected and the adjustment for error. To some, a presentation that understates the results is a breath of fresh air. Management reaction is often positive, so much so that it can become a detriment. When management reacts favorably to estimates, there may be a tendency not to use the more credible processes. Avoiding the use of more credible methods can be a mistake.

The Wisdom of Crowds

One of the most significant publications focusing on the power of collective input from average people is *The Wisdom of Crowds: Why the Many Are Smarter Than the Few and How Collective Wisdom Shapes Business, Economies, Societies, and Nations* (Surowiecki, 2004). The book begins with a story about British scientist Francis Galton, who, in 1906, left his home in the town of Plymouth and headed for a country fair. He was eighty-five years old. The story explains that Galton had devoted much of his career to measuring characteristics in breeding. His belief was that breeding mattered—that only a few people had the breeding necessary to keep the society healthy. As the story unfolds, Galton finds himself attending a weight-judging competition at which the audience would guess the weight of a fat ox after it had been slaughtered and dressed. Galton's theory of breeding told him that only the experts could make an accurate guess; however, there he stood, observing 800 ordinary people, mostly commoners, purchasing tickets on which they would place their guesses. Each person completed a ticket with his or her name, occupation, address, and estimate.

Galton wanted to prove that the average voter was capable of very little, so he turned his observation into an experiment. When the contest was over and the prizes had been awarded, Galton borrowed the tickets from the organizers and ran a series of statistical tests on them. Galton arranged the guesses (totaling 787—thirteen were discarded because they were illegible) in order from highest to lowest and graphed them to see if they would form a bell curve. Expecting the crowd members to be way off the mark, he added all their estimates, and calculated the mean. In so doing, he proved himself wrong. The crowd had guessed that the slaughtered and dressed ox would weigh 1,197 pounds. In actuality, it weighed 1,198 pounds. "In other words, the crowd's judgment was essentially perfect. The 'experts' were not close."

This simple story presents an example of the power of groups of people—and their estimates. As Surowiecki (2004) explains, what Francis Galton stumbled on that day in Plymouth was this simple but powerful truth: under the right circumstances, groups are remarkably intelligent and are often smarter than the smartest people in them. Groups do not need to be dominated by exceptionally intelligent people to be smart. Even if most of the people within a group are not especially well informed or rational, they can still reach a collectively wise decision.

Key Issues in Using Estimates

In summary, here are a few guidelines for effective use of estimates:

1. Estimates should be used as the technique of last resort for isolating program effects. When more credible methods are not appropriate for the situation, be prepared to use estimates and defend them.

2. Always use the most credible source of data; in many situations, that source is the participants. Be careful about obtaining data from the immediate managers of the participants; they may not be able to isolate the effects of different factors on performance.

3. Collect data in an unbiased way, ensuring that participants feel free to express their true feelings about how the effects of the program and other factors should be reported.

4. Collect data in the most effective way. The focus group process usually works best. When a focus group is not feasible or appropriate, interviews may be a workable option. As a last resort, collect the data by using questionnaires, adding key questions to capture the isolation data.

5. Adjust for error by collecting a confidence estimate (expressed as a percentage) from each participant and multiplying it by the allocation percentage. The confidence level serves as an error discount factor, allowing you to remove the error inherent in the estimation process.

6. Report the data carefully, explaining to management why estimation is being used and that it may not be completely accurate but that the value of the measured improvement has been adjusted in two ways: (1) only a portion of it has been attributed to the program, and (2) it has been adjusted to remove the error introduced through the estimation process.

Final Thoughts

This chapter discusses the use of estimates, perhaps the most unsettling and controversial yet nonetheless powerful technique for isolating the effects of a program. When more credible methods cannot be used, the fallback method is the use of estimates. While they represent the weakest method, estimates can still be accurate and credible if they are collected appropriately and adjusted for error. When estimation becomes commonplace or readily accepted, there is a danger that it will be preferred over more credible techniques, which is not recommended.

References

Phillips, P. P., and Phillips, J. J. *Proving the Value of HR: ROI Case Studies.* Birmingham, Ala.: ROI Institute, 2007.

Surowiecki, J. *The Wisdom of Crowds: Why the Many Are Smarter Than the Few and How Collective Wisdom Shapes Business, Economies, Societies, and Nations.* New York: Doubleday, 2004.

Use of Isolation Techniques

This chapter provides summary information and advice about using the different techniques for isolating the effects of programs. The chapter also includes exercises to ensure understanding of the use of the different methods.

Matching Exercise: Isolating the Effects of a Program

Perhaps it would be helpful to review some of the techniques by participating in an exercise.

Instructions

For each of the following situations, please indicate the best method for isolating the effects of the program. Select from these methods:

A. Control group
B. Trend line analysis
C. Forecasting
D. Participant's estimate
E. Use of customer input
F. Expert's estimate

In each box, write the letter that corresponds to the method used.

Situation	Method

1. A manufacturing company has recently implemented a new incentive plan to boost sales for client partners. Just as the plan was implemented, the company increased its promotional budget for each product line. Both the sales incentive plan and the sales promotion have driven an increase in sales. It appears that no other factors have contributed to this increase. Historical data show a mathematical relationship between the promotional budget and sales. This equation has been used to predict the sales increase, based on the increase in the promotional budget. This forecast is compared with actual figures to isolate the impact of the sales incentive program.

2. Absenteeism of bus drivers in a large metropolitan area had been a deteriorating situation for some time. A human resources program that included a no-fault absence policy and a change in the selection process was implemented. After the program was conducted, the rate of absenteeism decreased. No other influences appear to have contributed to the decrease. The pre-program data on absenteeism are very stable, and a trend was projected for the post-program period to compare with the actual figures. The difference between the projection and the actual figure represents the contribution of the project.

3. An agent training program in a real estate firm was designed to increase listings by teaching agents how to improve their presentation skills. Customers are asked to provide their rationale for deciding to list a home with a particular agent. Three months after the training program was completed, listings increased.

Situation	Method

Many factors caused the increase; however, according to customer feedback, one factor was the quality of the presentation made by the agent, which was the basis of the program. This information was used to understand the impact of the agent training program on the actual number of houses listed.

4. One year after an energy company opened a new wellness and fitness center for employees, the company's health care expenditures decreased. Given the amount of the decrease, the staff assembled several experts who could understand why health care costs have changed. These individuals have been asked to explain all the contributing factors and isolate the effects of the wellness and fitness center on that measure. □

5. A large automobile company implemented a sales consulting process on a pilot basis. Twelve dealerships were used in the initial pilot program. A comparison group of twelve other dealerships was selected against which to judge performance on several measures: sales volume, economy in the market, the sales versus service mix, incentives provided to sales staff, and the quality rating of the dealership. The difference between the two groups shows the impact of the sales consulting. □

6. In a leadership development program for a biotech company, the participating managers were asked to provide details on the impact of their use of leadership skills, using actual data from their work unit. As part of the exercise, the participants estimated the percentage of improvement that was directly related to the leadership development program. □

Responses

1. C. The mathematical relationship between sales, the program measure, and another factor, the promotional budget, makes forecasting possible.

2. B. The trend line of the rate of absenteeism can be projected on the basis of the pre-program data.

3. E. Customers can recognize a presentation's effectiveness, which stems directly from the training program.

4. F. Experts may be able to figure out what factors they think contributed to the improvement, although it would be a rare feat for outsiders to accomplish this.

5. A. This is a classic control group arrangement, the most effective method of isolating program effects.

6. D. Participants estimate the improvement generated by the program. Participant estimation will be the dominant method in many evaluations.

Case Study: National Computer Company

This case study shows how different methods for isolating program effects evolve as more credible methods are pursued or considered.

National Computer Company (NCC) sells computers to businesses and consumers. To ensure that customer service and support were sufficient, NCC established customer care centers in six geographic regions. All of the care centers were similar in size and employee characteristics. In recent years, NCC care centers had experienced a high employee turnover rate. To reduce turnover, a new program was developed to help managers improve employee engagement, appreciate employee concerns and differences, and communicate with employees effectively. NCC decided to implement this new program in one customer care center and compare the results with others.

Figure 5.1. Turnover Trend at the National Computer Company

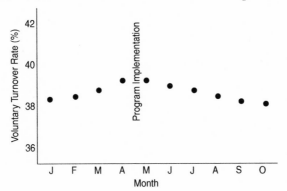

The NCC program staff decided that, for a variety of reasons, the customer care centers did not match appropriately. As a result, the control group arrangement for isolating program effects would not work. Therefore, projecting a data trend was considered. Figure 5.1 shows the trend of the annual turnover rate (reported monthly) during the four months before the program and the six months after the program.

In considering the impact of the new program on employee turnover, the staff identified an additional factor that was driving improvement. This factor was the change in the unemployment rate. In the area of the customer care center where the program was implemented, the unemployment rate increased from 5 percent to 6 percent. Figure 5.2 shows the relationship between the unemployment rate and the voluntary turnover rate. The mathematical relationship is $y = 50 - 3x$, where x is the unemployment rate and y is the voluntary turnover rate. As the unemployment rate increased from 5 percent to 6 percent, the turnover rate went down. The mathematical relationship between the unemployment rate and the turnover rate can be used to estimate how much of the reduced turnover was caused by the increased unemployment rate, not the program. When no other factors are involved other

Figure 5.2. Relationship Between Unemployment and Voluntary Turnover

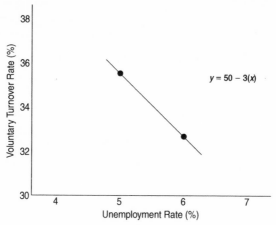

than the program, the improvement in turnover rate not allocated to increased unemployment is attributed to the program

However, after further examination, it was determined that not only was the unemployment rate increasing, resulting in lower turnover, but that other key factors were contributing to the turnover. First, the customer care management team placed emphasis on this issue, working diligently with employees and team leaders to make the organization a more attractive place to work, to understand the problems that might lead to an employee's departure, and to avoid turnover, if possible. This emphasis on reducing turnover had had an impact on the turnover rate. In addition, one of NCC's competitors in the local market that had often recruited employees from NCC customer care was experiencing a downturn and laying off employees. This development had minimized opportunities at the competitor company, stopped the recruiting, and contributed to the reduction in turnover. In essence, turnover was reduced by three factors in addition to the program designed to improve the skills and capabilities of the management team. As a result, a decision was made to use estimates from team leaders as a

Table 5.1. One Team Leader's View of Factors Contributing to Turnover

Contributing Factors	Impact on Results	Confidence Level
Program	30%	80%
Unemployment rate	50%	100%
Management emphasis	5%	70%
Competition	15%	90%

technique for isolating the effects of the program. Table 5.1 shows an example of one team leader's evaluation of the four factors that affected turnover at NCC.

Why Isolation Is a Key Issue

Isolating the effects of a program on business impact data is one of the most challenging steps in the ROI Methodology, yet it is essential. When addressed credibly, this step links learning directly to business impact.

Other Factors Are Always There

In almost every situation, multiple factors create business results. The world does not just stand still while programs are implemented. Many functions in an organization may be attempting to improve the same metrics. A situation in which no other factors enter into the process is almost impossible.

Without It, There Is No Business Link: Evidence Versus Proof

Without taking steps to show the contribution, there is no business linkage—only evidence that the program could have made a difference. Results have improved; however, other factors may have influenced the data. The proof that the program has made a difference on the business measure comes from this step in the process—isolating the effects of the program.

Other Factors and Influences Have Protective Owners

The owners of the other processes that influence results are convinced that their processes made the difference. For example, employees in marketing, technology, and quality functions are convinced that improvements are entirely due to their efforts. They present a compelling case to management, stressing their achievements. In real situations, other processes, such as performance improvement, reward systems, and job redesign, also have protective owners, and they often are convinced and are prepared to convince others that they made the difference.

To Do It Right Is Not Easy

The challenge of isolating the effects of a program on impact data is critical and can be achieved, but it is not an easy process for complex programs, especially when strong-willed owners of other processes are involved. Determination is needed to address this situation every time an ROI evaluation is conducted. Fortunately, a variety of approaches are available, as has been shown in this book.

Without It, the Study Is Not Valid

A study is not valid unless it addresses the issue of isolation of program effects, because other factors are almost always in the mix, so a direct connection to the program is not apparent. In any study, three things should never be done by an evaluator:

1. Taking all the credit for the improvement without addressing the issue of isolating the program's effects

2. Doing nothing, attempting to ignore the critical issue of isolation

3. Admitting that he or she does not have the knowledge to address the issue of how to isolate the program's effects

Doing any of these things will lower the credibility of the case for the program's connection to business improvement.

Isolation Myths

Several myths about isolating the effects of a program often create concerns, confusion, and frustration with the process. Some researchers, professionals, and consultants inflame the situation by suggesting that isolating program effects is not necessary. Here are the most common myths:

1. *Most programs are complementary with other processes; therefore, an attempt to isolate the effects of a program should not be made.* New initiatives complement other factors, all of which drive results. However, if the sponsor of a program needs to understand the relative contribution of that program, this issue must be tackled. If accomplished properly, it will show how all the complementary factors work together to drive the improvements.

2. *Other functions in the organization do not isolate the effects of their programs, so we don't need to either.* While managers in some functions avoid this issue and try to make a convincing case that all improvement is related to their own processes, others are effectively addressing the issue of demonstrating that their programs produce tangible results. Using a credible approach to address this issue is necessary if the linkage to results is to be perceived as likely. Many organizations ask customers to complete

a customer survey after they make a purchase or open a new account. These organizations usually ask customers why they made their purchases. The organizations are trying to isolate the effects of multiple variables that influence why customers make purchases.

3. *If a control group analysis cannot be used, then no attempt to isolate the effects of the program should be made.* Although a control group analysis is the most credible approach, it will not be feasible in the majority of situations. As a result, other methods must be used to isolate program effects. The problem does not go away just because a desired or favorite technique cannot be used. The challenge is to find other processes that are effective and that will work anytime, even if they are not as credible as the control group method.

4. *The stakeholders will understand the link; therefore, an attempt to isolate the effects of a program on impact measures is not necessary.* Unfortunately, stakeholders see and understand what is presented to them. Absence of information makes understanding the link difficult for them, especially when others are claiming full credit for the improvement.

5. *Estimates of improvement provide no value.* Although the use of estimates is a choice of last resort for isolating program effects, it can provide value and be a credible process, particularly when the estimates are adjusted for error. Using estimates from the individuals who best understand the process is certainly better than not isolating program effects at all. Estimates are used routinely to isolate the effects of programs in many organizations.

6. *If we ignore the issue of isolating program effects, maybe management won't think about it.* Unfortunately, audiences are becoming more sophisticated on this issue, and they are aware of multiple influences. If no attempt is made to isolate the effects of a program, the audience will assume that the other factors have

had a tremendous effect—perhaps, all the effect. As a result, the credibility of the program will deteriorate.

———————

These myths underscore the importance of tackling the issue of isolating program effects. All of this is not to suggest that a specific program is not implemented in harmony with other processes. All groups should work as a team to produce the desired results. However, when funding is provided to different functions in the organization—with different process owners—there is always a struggle to show and, sometimes even to understand, the connection between the programs of each function and the results. If the issue is not addressed by the program team, others will address it, leaving the program owners with less-than-desired budgets, resources, and respect.

Build Credibility with the Isolation Process

Several items must be addressed in regard to credibility. This step—isolation of program effects—is the most significant credibility issue in the ROI Methodology.

Selecting the Technique

Table 5.2 shows the frequency with which isolation techniques are used by over two hundred organizations that have been applying the ROI Methodology for five years or more. The table shows a high percentage for control group analysis; the use of this method in all impact studies would be lower. After all, the organizations represented in Table 5.2 are the best-practice organizations, and they have worked diligently to use the most credible analyses. "Other" encompasses a variety of techniques that are less likely to be used.

Table 5.2. Use of Techniques for Isolating Program Effects in Best-Practice Organizations

Technique[1]	Frequency of Use[2]
Control group analysis	35%
Trend line analysis or forecasting	20%
Expert estimation	50%
Other	20%

[1]Techniques are listed in order of credibility.
[2]Percentages exceed 100% because some organizations use more than one technique.

With several techniques available to isolate the impact of a program, selecting the most appropriate method (or methods) for a specific program can be difficult. Estimates are simple and inexpensive, while other techniques are more time-consuming and costly. When selecting an isolation technique, consider these factors:

- Feasibility of the technique

- Accuracy provided by the technique, compared to the accuracy needed

- Credibility of the technique with the target audience

- Cost of implementing the technique

- Amount of disruption of normal work activities that will result from implementation of the technique

- Participant, staff, and management time needed to implement the technique

Using Multiple Methods

Multiple isolation techniques or sources of data input should be considered, because two sources are usually better than one. When multiple sources are used, it is recommended that a conservative method be used to combine the inputs—for example, using the results that are least favorable to the program. A conservative approach builds acceptance and credibility. The target audience should always be provided with explanations of the process and the various subjective factors involved. Multiple sources allow an organization to experiment with different methods and build confidence with a particular technique. For example, if management is concerned about the accuracy of the participants' estimates, a combination of a control group arrangement and participants' estimates could be used to check the accuracy of the estimation process.

Building Credibility

It is not unusual for the ROI for a program to be extremely large. Even when a portion of the improvement is allocated to other factors, in many situations the numbers are still impressive. The audience should understand that although every effort was made to isolate the program's impact, it is still a figure that may not be precise and may contain error. It represents the best estimate of the program's impact, given the constraints, conditions, and resources available.

One way to strengthen the credibility of the ROI is to consider the different factors that influence the credibility of data. Exhibit 5.1 lists factors that typically influence the credibility of data

---

Exhibit 5.1. Issues That Affect the Credibility of Data

- Reputation of the source of the data
- Motives of the researchers
- Personal bias of audience
- Methodology of the study
- Assumptions made in the analysis
- Realism of the outcome data
- Type of data
- Scope of analysis

---

presented to a particular group. The issue of isolating the effects of a program is influenced by several of these credibility factors. First, the reputation of the source of the data is critical. The most knowledgeable expert must provide input and be involved in the analysis. The motives of the researchers can also be a critical issue. For example, to increase credibility, a third party should facilitate any focus group that is completed and the data must be collected in an objective way. The personal biases of the audience members can make a difference, and steps should be taken to alleviate concerns that might arise from known biases in the audience. Also, the assumptions made in the analysis and in the methodology of the study should be clearly defined so that the audience will understand the steps that were taken to increase credibility. The type of data may affect how credible it is perceived to be. Managers prefer to deal with hard data that can be linked to the direct output of a program. Finally, by isolating the effects of only one program, the scope of analysis is kept narrow, enhancing credibility.

Final Thoughts

This chapter reviews the variety of methods that can be used to isolate the effects of programs. These techniques represent the most effective ways to address this issue and are used by some of the most progressive organizations. Too often, results are reported and linked to a program without any attempt to isolate the portion of the results that can be attributed to the program. This chapter also discusses issues pertaining to the necessity of performing this step and how to maximize the credibility of the analysis.

Index

A

Advertising–daily sale relationship forecast, 51–53

Alliger, G. M., 9

Armstrong, J., 53

B

Basic control group design, 17–18

Brinkerhoff, R. O., 6

C

Case studies

Crack Box, Inc., 87–89

Federal Information Agency (FIA), 34–36

First Bank, 2–5

Global Financial Services, Inc. (GFS), 85–87

Healthcare, Inc. (HI), 54–57

International Software Company, 41–43

Micro Electronics, 53–54

Midwest Electric, Inc., 36–40

Multi-National, Inc., 90–92

National Bank, 76–80

National Book Company, 57–59

National Computer Company (NCC), 102–105

Public Bank of Malaysia, 89–90

Retail Merchandise Company (RMC), 31–34

Chain of impact, 7, 8–10

Contaminated control groups, 25–26

Control group design

basic, 17–18

deciding which design to select, 21

ideal experimental, 18–20

posttest-only, 20–21

threats to validity of, 15–17

Control group issues

ethical considerations, 23–24

feasibility as, 29–31

FSI case example of potential problems, 24–29

practicality as, 22–23

viability as, 22

Control groups

designing, 15–21

Federal Information Agency (FIA) example of, 34–36

frequency of use for isolating effects, 109–110

International Software Company (ISC) example of, 41–43

as isolating program effects technique, 6, 7–8

isolation myth regarding use of, 108

issues when considering, 22–31

Midwest Electric, Inc. example of, 36–40

Control groups (*Continued*)
  National Computer Company
    (NCC) example of, 102–103
  Retail Merchandise Company
    (RMC) example of, 31–34
  See also Participants
Crack Box, Inc. case study, 87–89
Customer expert estimates, 6, 83,
  94–95

D
Data
  building credibility regarding,
    111–114
  control groups, 6, 7–8, 15–44
  expert estimates, 6, 61–97
  forecast method for, 6, 50–53
  issues that affect credibility of, 114
  trend line analysis, 6, 45, 46–50,
    53–59
Dou, Z., 15
Dressler, D., 6

E
Ethical control group issue, 23–24
Expert estimates
  Crack Box, Inc. example of, 87–89
  of customers, 6, 83
  demonstrating power of, 92–93
  of focus groups, 63–66, 94–95
  frequency of use for isolating
    effects, 110
  Global Financial Services, Inc.
    (GFS) example of, 85–87
  of immediate managers, 80–82, 94
  isolating program effects using, 6,
    61–62, 84
  key issues in using, 95–96
  Multi-National, Inc. example of,
    90–92
  National Computer Company
    (NCC) example of, 104–105
  of participants, 62–80, 93–94
  Public Bank of Malaysia example
    of, 89–90

research on power of, 92
  of senior management, 82–83, 94

F
Feasibility control group issue,
  29–31
Federal Information Agency (FIA)
  case study, 34–36
Financial Services, Inc. (FSI),
  24–26
First Bank case study, 2–5
Focus groups
  participant estimates from, 63–64
  steps for most credible estimates
    from, 64–66
  validity of estimates by, 94–95
  See also Participants
Forecast method
  advertising–daily sales
    relationship example of, 51–52
  described, 45–46
  disadvantages of, 52–53
  frequency of use for isolating
    effects, 110
  isolating program effects using, 6
  linear model of, 50
  National Computer Company
    (NCC) example of, 102–105

G
Glaton, F., 94–95
Global Financial Services, Inc.
  (GFS) case study, 85–87

H
Healthcare, Inc. (HI) case study,
  54–57
Hotel staff turnover trend line
  analysis, 48–49

I
Ideal experimental control group
  design, 18–20
Immediate manager estimates,
  80–82, 94

Impact of other factors, 10–12, 84–85
Improvement
  First Bank case study identifying reasons for, 2–5
  identifying other factors contributing to, 10–12
  isolating program effects to identify reasons for, 1–12
  isolation myth regarding, 108
International Software Company (ISC) case study, 41–43
Interviews, 74
Isolating program effects
  building credibility regarding, 109–112
  First Bank case study showing importance of, 2–5
  matching exercise for, 99–102
  myths related to, 107–109
  preliminary issues in, 5–12
  recognizing importance of, 1, 105–107
  required to understand program's impact, 2
  See also Programs
Isolating program effects issues
  identifying chain of impact, 8–10
  identifying factors other than program, 10–12, 84–85
  need to isolate program effects, 6–8
Isolating program effects techniques
  control groups, 6, 7–8, 15–44, 102–103, 108, 110
  expert estimates, 6, 61–97, 104–105, 108
  forecast method, 6, 50–53, 110
  frequency of use of specific, 110
  listed, 6
  National Computer Company (NCC) case study on different, 102–105
  using multiple, 110–111

selecting the right, 109–110
trend line analysis, 6, 45, 46–50, 53–59, 103, 112

J
Janak, E. A., 9

K
Kaufman, R., 10
Keuler, D., 22

L
Lee, N., 15

M
Management
  expert estimates from immediate, 80–82, 94
  expert estimates from senior, 82–83, 94
  isolation myth regarding, 108–109
Matching exercise, 99–102
Micro Electronics case study, 53–54
Midwest Electric, Inc., case study, 36–40
Mortality of participants, 16
Multi-National, Inc., case study, 90–92

N
National Bank case study, 76–80
National Book Company case study, 57–59
National Computer Company (NCC) case study
  using control group, 103
  using expert estimates, 104–105
  using mathematical forecasting, 103–104
  using trend line analysis, 103

O
Other factors impact, 10–12, 84–85

P

Participants
advantages/disadvantages of
estimates from, 75–76
expert estimates from, 62–80,
93–94
interviews to obtain estimates
from, 74
mortality of, 16
National Bank case study on
estimates from, 76–80
questionnaires to obtain estimates
from, 68–74
testing effects on, 16
See also Control groups; Focus
groups
Phillips, J. J., 22, 34, 36, 40, 57,
89
Phillips, P. P., 22, 34, 36, 40, 57,
89
Posttest-only control group design,
20–21
Practicality issue, 22–23
Preskill, H., 6
Programs
identifying chain of impact, 7,
8–10
identifying contribution of, 7
impact of factors other than,
10–12, 84–85
isolating program effects for
understanding impact of, 2
See also Isolating program effects
Proving the Value of HR: ROI Case
Studies (Phillips and Phillips),
34, 36, 40, 57, 89
Public Bank of Malaysia case study,
89–90

Q

Questionnaires
examples of questions used in,
69–70
Guiding Principles used to create,
72–73
participant estimates using,
68–74
sample of input from, 71

R

Retail Merchandise Company
(RMC) case study, 31–34
ROI Guiding Principles
for immediate managers'
estimates, 81
for participant estimate
questionnaire, 72–73
ROI Methodology
Guiding Principles of, 72–73, 81
isolation as credibility issue in,
109–112
isolation as key issue for,
105–107
Russ-Eft, D., 6

S

Sale revenue trend line analysis,
47–48
Salkind, N., 48
Senior management estimates,
82–83, 94
Sexual harassment trend line
analysis, 54–57
Shipment productivity trend line
analysis, 57–59
Stakeholder isolation myth, 108
Surowiecki, J., 94, 95

T

Testing effects, 16
Time issue, 16
Trend line analysis
conditions required for, 46, 49
described, 45–46
frequency of use for isolating
effects, 110
guidelines for working with,
49–50
Healthcare, Inc. (HI) example of,
54–57

hotel staff turnover example of,
    48–49
isolating program effects using, 6
Micro Electronics example of,
    53–54
National Book Company example
    of, 57–59
National Computer Company
    (NCC) example of, 103–104
sale revenue example of, 47–48
True experimental control group
    design, 18

V
Validity
    isolating program effects for study,
        109
    threats to control group, 15–17
Verizon Communications, 22
Viability issue, 22

W
Wang, G., 15
The Wisdom of Crowds:
    (Surowiecki), 94

About the Authors

Jack J. Phillips, Ph.D., a world-renowned expert on accountability, measurement, and evaluation, provides consulting services for Fortune 500 companies and major global organizations. The author or editor of more than fifty books, Phillips conducts workshops and makes conference presentations throughout the world.

His expertise in measurement and evaluation is based on more than twenty-seven years of corporate experience in the aerospace, textile, metals, construction materials, and banking industries. Phillips has served as training and development manager at two Fortune 500 firms, as senior human resources officer at two firms, as president of a regional bank, and as management professor at a major state university. This background led Phillips to develop the ROI Methodology, a revolutionary process that provides bottom-line figures and accountability for all types of learning, performance improvement, human resources, technology, and public policy programs.

Phillips regularly consults with clients in manufacturing, service, and government organizations in forty-four countries in North and South America, Europe, Africa, Australia, and Asia.

Books most recently authored by Phillips include *Show Me the Money: How to Determine ROI in People, Projects, and Programs* (Berrett-Koehler, 2007); *The Value of Learning* (Pfeiffer,

2007); *How to Build a Successful Consulting Practice* (McGraw-Hill, 2006); *Investing in Your Company's Human Capital: Strategies to Avoid Spending Too Much or Too Little* (Amacom, 2005); *Proving the Value of HR: How and Why to Measure ROI* (Society for Human Resource Management, 2005); *The Leadership Scorecard* (Butterworth-Heinemann, 2004); *Managing Employee Retention* (Butterworth-Heinemann, 2003); *Return on Investment in Training and Performance Improvement Programs*, 2nd edition (Butterworth-Heinemann, 2003); *The Project Management Scorecard* (Butterworth-Heinemann, 2002); *How to Measure Training Results* (McGraw-Hill, 2002); *The Human Resources Scorecard: Measuring the Return on Investment* (Butterworth-Heinemann, 2001); *The Consultant's Scorecard* (McGraw-Hill, 2000); and *Performance Analysis and Consulting* (ASTD, 2000). Phillips served as series editor for the In Action casebook series of the American Society for Training and Development (ASTD), an ambitious publishing project featuring thirty titles. He currently serves as series editor for Butterworth-Heinemann's Improving Human Performance series and for Pfeiffer's new Measurement and Evaluation series.

Phillips has received several awards for his books and his work. The Society for Human Resource Management presented him with an award for one of his books and honored a Phillips ROI study with its highest award for creativity. ASTD gave him its highest award, Distinguished Contribution to Workplace Learning and Development. *Meeting News* named Phillips one of the twenty-five most influential people in the meetings and events industry, based on his work on ROI within the industry.

Phillips holds undergraduate degrees in electrical engineering, physics, and mathematics; a master's degree in decision sciences from Georgia State University; and a Ph.D. degree in human resources management from the University of Alabama.

Jack Phillips has served on the boards of several private businesses—including two NASDAQ companies—and several associations, including ASTD, and nonprofit organizations. He is

chairman of the ROI Institute, Inc., and can be reached at
(205) 678-8101, or by e-mail at jack@roiinstitute.net.

Bruce C. Aaron, Ph.D., is responsible for research and evaluation
of learning and knowledge management initiatives within Accenture, a global management consulting, technology services, and
outsourcing company. During his tenure, Accenture Education has
received several awards from professional associations for excel-
lence in measurement and evaluation, including the 2004 ASTD
ROI Impact Study of the Year award.

Bruce joined Accenture in 1998 after several years as a public sector evaluation consultant for district and state educational
agencies in Florida. He has presented to a wide range of professional audiences for organizations such as the International Society
for Performance Improvement (ISPI), ASTD, SALT, American
Educational Research Association (AERA), and the Psychometric
Society on topics in statistics, measurement, evaluation, instructional technology, and group decision-making systems.

Bruce has authored and coauthored dozens of papers, presentations, articles, and books. He has recently coauthored *Return
on Learning, Part 4: Maximizing the Business Impact of Enterprise
Learning* (Accenture, 2007), *Handbook of Research on Electronic
Surveys and Measurements* (IGI Publishing, 2007), and a chapter
in *Instructional Design in the Real World: A View from the Trenches*
(Information Science Publishing, 2004).

Bruce has served on the advisory committee for the ASTD ROI
Network, and is a certified professional in learning and performance
(CPLP). He received his M.A. degree in school psychology and his
Ph.D. degree in educational measurement and evaluation from the
University of South Florida.

Pfeiffer Publications Guide

This guide is designed to familiarize you with the various types of Pfeiffer publications. The formats section describes the various types of products that we publish; the methodologies section describes the many different ways that content might be provided within a product. We also provide a list of the topic areas in which we publish.

FORMATS

In addition to its extensive book-publishing program, Pfeiffer offers content in an array of formats, from fieldbooks for the practitioner to complete, ready-to-use training packages that support group learning.

FIELDBOOK Designed to provide information and guidance to practitioners in the midst of action. Most fieldbooks are companions to another, sometimes earlier, work, from which its ideas are derived; the fieldbook makes practical what was theoretical in the original text. Fieldbooks can certainly be read from cover to cover. More likely, though, you'll find yourself bouncing around following a particular theme, or dipping in as the mood, and the situation, dictate.

HANDBOOK A contributed volume of work on a single topic, comprising an eclectic mix of ideas, case studies, and best practices sourced by practitioners and experts in the field.

An editor or team of editors usually is appointed to seek out contributors and to evaluate content for relevance to the topic. Think of a handbook not as a ready-to-eat meal, but as a cookbook of ingredients that enables you to create the most fitting experience for the occasion.

RESOURCE Materials designed to support group learning. They come in many forms: a complete, ready-to-use exercise (such as a game); a comprehensive resource on one topic (such as conflict management) containing a variety of methods and approaches; or a collection of like-minded activities (such as icebreakers) on multiple subjects and situations.

TRAINING PACKAGE An entire, ready-to-use learning program that focuses on a particular topic or skill. All packages comprise a guide for the facilitator/trainer and a workbook for the participants. Some packages are supported with additional media—such as video—or learning aids, instruments, or other devices to help participants understand concepts or practice and develop skills.

- *Facilitator/trainer's guide* Contains an introduction to the program, advice on how to organize and facilitate the learning event, and step-by-step instructor notes. The guide also contains copies of presentation materials—handouts, presentations, and overhead designs, for example—used in the program.

- *Participant's workbook* Contains exercises and reading materials that support the learning goal and serves as a valuable reference and support guide for participants in the weeks and months that follow the learning event. Typically, each participant will require his or her own workbook.

ELECTRONIC CD-ROMs and web-based products transform static Pfeiffer content into dynamic, interactive experiences. Designed to take advantage of the searchability, automation, and ease-of-use that technology provides, our e-products bring convenience and immediate accessibility to your workspace.

METHODOLOGIES

CASE STUDY A presentation, in narrative form, of an actual event that has occurred inside an organization. Case studies are not prescriptive, nor are they used to prove a point; they are designed to develop critical analysis and decision-making skills. A case study has a specific time frame, specifies a sequence of events, is narrative in structure, and contains a plot structure—an issue (what should be/have been done?). Use case studies when the goal is to enable participants to apply previously learned theories to the circumstances in the case, decide what is pertinent, identify the real issues, decide what should have been done, and develop a plan of action.

ENERGIZER A short activity that develops readiness for the next session or learning event. Energizers are most commonly used after a break or lunch to stimulate or refocus the group. Many involve some form of physical activity, so they are a useful way to counter post-lunch lethargy. Other uses include transitioning from one topic to another, where "mental" distancing is important.

EXPERIENTIAL LEARNING ACTIVITY (ELA) A facilitator-led intervention that moves participants through the learning cycle from experience to application (also known as a Structured Experience). ELAs are carefully thought-out designs in which there is a definite learning purpose and intended outcome. Each step—everything that participants do during the activity— facilitates the accomplishment of the stated goal. Each ELA includes complete instructions for facilitating the intervention and a clear statement of goals, suggested group size and timing, materials required, an explanation of the process, and, where appropriate, possible variations to the activity. (For more detail on Experiential Learning Activities, see the Introduction to the *Reference Guide to Handbooks and Annuals*, 1999 edition, Pfeiffer, San Francisco.)

GAME A group activity that has the purpose of fostering team spirit and togetherness in addition to the achievement of a pre-stated goal. Usually contrived—undertaking a desert expedition, for example—this type of learning method offers an engaging means for participants to demonstrate and practice business and interpersonal skills. Games are effective for team building and personal development mainly because the goal is subordinate to the process—the means through which participants reach decisions, collaborate, communicate, and generate trust and understanding. Games often engage teams in "friendly" competition.

ICEBREAKER A (usually) short activity designed to help participants overcome initial anxiety in a training session and/or to acquaint the participants with one another. An icebreaker can be a fun activity or can be tied to specific topics or training goals. While a useful tool in itself, the icebreaker comes into its own in situations where tension or resistance exists within a group.

INSTRUMENT A device used to assess, appraise, evaluate, describe, classify, and summarize various aspects of human behavior. The term used to describe an instrument depends primarily on its format and purpose. These terms include survey, questionnaire, inventory, diagnostic, survey, and poll. Some uses of instruments include providing instrumental feedback to group members, studying here-and-now processes or functioning within a group, manipulating group composition, and evaluating outcomes of training and other interventions.

Instruments are popular in the training and HR field because, in general, more growth can occur if an individual is provided with a method for focusing specifically on his or her own behavior. Instruments also are used to obtain information that will serve as a basis for change and to assist in workforce planning efforts.

Paper-and-pencil tests still dominate the instrument landscape with a typical package comprising a facilitator's guide, which offers advice on administering the instrument and interpreting the collected data, and an initial set of instruments. Additional instruments are available separately. Pfeiffer, though, is investing heavily in e-instruments. Electronic instrumentation provides effortless distribution and, for larger groups particularly, offers advantages over paper-and-pencil tests in the time it takes to analyze data and provide feedback.

LECTURETTE A short talk that provides an explanation of a principle, model, or process that is pertinent to the participants' current learning needs. A lecturette is intended to establish a common language bond between the trainer and the participants by providing a mutual frame of reference. Use a lecturette as an introduction to a group activity or event, as an interjection during an event, or as a handout.

MODEL A graphic depiction of a system or process and the relationship among its elements. Models provide a frame of reference and something more tangible, and more easily remembered, than a verbal explanation. They also give participants something to "go on," enabling them to track their own progress as they experience the dynamics, processes, and relationships being depicted in the model.

ROLE PLAY A technique in which people assume a role in a situation/ scenario: a customer service rep in an angry-customer exchange, for example. The way in which the role is approached is then discussed and feedback is offered. The role play is often repeated using a different approach and/or incorporating changes made based on feedback received. In other words, role playing is a spontaneous interaction involving realistic behavior under artificial (and safe) conditions.

SIMULATION A methodology for understanding the interrelationships among components of a system or process. Simulations differ from games in that they test or use a model that depicts or mirrors some aspect of reality in form, if not necessarily in content. Learning occurs by studying the effects of change on one or more factors of the model. Simulations are commonly used to test hypotheses about what happens in a system—often referred to as "what if?" analysis—or to examine best-case/worst-case scenarios.

THEORY A presentation of an idea from a conjectural perspective. Theories are useful because they encourage us to examine behavior and phenomena through a different lens.

TOPICS

The twin goals of providing effective and practical solutions for workforce training and organization development and meeting the educational needs of training and human resource professionals shape Pfeiffer's publishing program. Core topics include the following:

Leadership & Management

Communication & Presentation

Coaching & Mentoring

Training & Development

E-Learning

Teams & Collaboration

OD & Strategic Planning

Human Resources

Consulting

What will you find on pfeiffer.com?

- The best in workplace performance solutions for training and HR professionals

- Downloadable training tools, exercises, and content

- Web-exclusive offers

- Training tips, articles, and news

- Seamless on-line ordering

- Author guidelines, information on becoming a Pfeiffer Affiliate, and much more

Discover more at www.pfeiffer.com

Measurement and Evaluation Series

Series Editors
Patricia Pulliam Phillips, Ph.D., and Jack J. Phillips, Ph.D.

A six-book set that provides a step-by-step system for planning, measuring, calculating, and communicating evaluation and Return-on-Investment for training and development, featuring:

- Detailed templates
- Complete plans
- Ready-to-use tools
- Real-world case examples

The M&E Series features:

1. *ROI Fundamentals: Why and When to Measure ROI* (978-0-7879-8716-9)

2. *Data Collection: Planning For and Collecting All Types of Data* (978-0-7879-8718-3)

3. *Isolation of Results: Defining the Impact of the Program* (978-0-7879-8719-0)

4. *Data Conversion: Calculating the Monetary Benefits* (978-0-7879-8720-6)

5. *Costs and ROI: Evaluating at the Ultimate Level* (978-0-7879-8721-3)

6. *Communication and Implementation: Sustaining the Practice* (978-0-7879-8722-0)

Plus, the *ROI in Action Casebook* (978-0-7879-8717-6) covers all the major workplace learning and performance applications, including Leadership Development, Sales Training, Performance Improvement, Technical Skills Training, Information Technology Training, Orientation and OJT, and Supervisor Training.

The **ROI Methodology** is a comprehensive measurement and evaluation process that collects six types of measures: Reaction, Satisfaction, and Planned Action; Learning; Application and Implementation; Business Impact; Return on Investment; and Intangible Measures. The process provides a step-by-step system for evaluation and planning, data collection, data analysis, and reporting. It is appropriate for the measurement and evaluation of *all* kinds of performance improvement programs and activities, including training and development, learning, human resources, coaching, meetings and events, consulting, and project management.

Special Offer from the ROI Institute

Send for your own ROI Process Model, an indispensable tool for implementing and presenting ROI in your organization. The ROI Institute is offering an exclusive gift to readers of The Measurement and Evaluation Series. This 11"×25" multicolor foldout shows the ROI Methodology flow model and the key issues surrounding the implementation of the ROI Methodology. This easy-to-understand overview of the ROI Methodology has proven invaluable to countless professionals when implementing the ROI Methodology. Please return this page or e-mail your information to the address below to receive your free foldout (a $6.00 value). Please check your area(s) of interest in ROI.

Please send me the ROI Process Model described in the book. I am interested in learning more about the following ROI materials and services:

☐ Workshops and briefing on ROI   ☐ ROI consulting services
☐ Books and support materials on ROI   ☐ ROI Network information
☐ Certification in the ROI Methodology ☐ ROI benchmarking
☐ ROI software   ☐ ROI research

Name _____

Title _____

Organization _____

Address _____

Phone _____

E-mail Address _____

Functional area of interest:

☐ Learning and Development/Performance Improvement
☐ Human Resources/Human Capital
☐ Public Relations/Community Affairs/Government Relations
☐ Consulting
☐ Sales/Marketing
☐ Technology/IT Systems
☐ Project Management Solutions
☐ Quality/Six Sigma
☐ Operations/Methods/Engineering
☐ Research and Development/Innovations
☐ Finance/Compliance
☐ Logistics/Distribution/Supply Chain
☐ Public Policy Initiatives
☐ Social Programs
☐ Other (Please Specify) _____

Organizational Level

☐ executive   ☐ management ☐ consultant   ☐ specialist
☐ student   ☐ evaluator   ☐ researcher

Return this form or contact The ROI Institute
                             P.O. Box 380637
                             Birmingham, AL 35238-0637

Or e-mail information to info@roiinstitute.net
Please allow four to six weeks for delivery.